Do children have rights?

DATE DUE

At Issue

Do Children
Have Rights?

Other Books in the At Issue Series:

At Issue

Do Children Have Rights?

Christine Watkins, Book Editor

GREENHAVEN PRESS
A part of Gale, Cengage Learning

NEW ENGLAND INSTITUTE OF TECHNOLOGY
LIBRARY

GALE
CENGAGE Learning™

Detroit • New York • San Francisco • New Haven, Conn • Waterville, Maine • London

639573885

2\11

GALE
CENGAGE Learning™

Christine Nasso, *Publisher*
Elizabeth Des Chenes, *Managing Editor*

© 2011 Greenhaven Press, a part of Gale, Cengage Learning.

Gale and Greenhaven Press are registered trademarks used herein under license.

For more information, contact:
Greenhaven Press
27500 Drake Rd.
Farmington Hills, MI 48331-3535
Or you can visit our Internet site at gale.cengage.com

For product information and technology assistance, contact us at

Gale Customer Support, 1-800-877-4253
For permission to use material from this text or product, submit all requests online at www.cengage.com/permissions.

Further permissions questions can be e-mailed to permissionrequest@cengage.com.

Articles in Greenhaven Press anthologies are often edited for length to meet page require- ments. In addition, original titles of these works are changed to clearly present the main thesis and to explicitly indicate the author's opinion. Every effort is made to ensure that Greenhaven Press accurately reflects the original intent of the authors. Every effort has been made to trace the owners of copyrighted material.

Cover image © Images.com/Corbis.

LIBRARY OF CONGRESS CATALOGING-IN-PUBLICATION DATA

Do children have rights? / Christine Watkins, book editor.
    p. cm. -- (At issue)
  Includes bibliographical references and index.
  ISBN 978-0-7377-4876-5 (hardcover) -- ISBN 978-0-7377-4877-2 (pbk.)
  1. Children's rights--Juvenile literature. 2. Children--Legal status, laws, etc.-- Juvenile literature. 3. Child labor--Juvenile literature. 4. Sex instruction for children--Juvenile literature. I. Watkins, Christine, 1951-
  HQ789.D622 2010
  323.3'52--dc22

                                                 2010021987

Printed in the United States of America
1 2 3 4 5 6 7 14 13 12 11 10

Contents

Introduction

More than half a million children—some under the age of ten—have been recruited into armed forces in more than eighty-five countries worldwide, according to the Coalition to Stop the Use of Child Soldiers. And girls are not excluded; they are recruited as active combatants, in addition to roles as prostitutes, as sex slaves, and as "wives" for other combatants. Children are targeted because of their inexperience and vulnerability, making them more easily indoctrinated; if they resist, drugs are often used to break down any psychological barriers. Once recruited, these children can be subjected to brutal initiation rituals in which they are forced to kill or injure members of their own families, and youngsters are beaten or killed if they try to escape.

> When I was abducted in 2003, we had no food for three days. We lived only on water. . . . They [the rebels] told us to decide among ourselves who should be eaten. At first we thought it was a joke until they decided themselves on a certain girl whom they slaughtered and cut into pieces. Then they told us to cook the pieces. When it was ready, the rebels forced us to eat the cooked girl. After that we were told to kill an old man who was helpless. After a week, the rebels brought us to Amaseniko camp [in Amuria district in eastern Uganda], where we had been abducted, and told us to burn houses. I was told to kill my grandfather. When I tried to refuse, the rebels beat me hard until I accepted to kill him using heavy stones. Then we went ahead to kill two more people we came across.

This was recounted by a thirteen-year-old girl to researchers for the February 2008 report "Returning Home—Children's Perspectives on Reintegration: A Case Study of Children Abducted by the Lord's Resistance Army in Teso, Eastern Uganda," by the Coalition to Stop the Use of Child Soldiers.

Her story is just one of many. According to the United Nations Children's Fund (UNICEF), this "illegal and morally reprehensible practice" of using children as soldiers continues in many armed conflicts around the world, despite efforts by the international community to end it.

Such efforts to end the use of child soldiers include the Optional Protocol to the Convention on the Rights of the Child on the Involvement of Children in Armed Conflict set forth by the United Nations in 2002. It outlaws the recruitment or participation of anyone under the age of eighteen in insurgency groups, rebel forces, or government and nongovernment armed forces "under any circumstances." Almost two thirds of the world's states have ratified the Optional Protocol, and others prohibit the use of child soldiers through their own national or state laws. Additionally, the International Criminal Court now has the jurisdiction to investigate the recruitment and use of child soldiers, and new mechanisms to monitor and report abuses against children have been put in place, as well as initiatives to build awareness among armed groups about children's rights. And for children who have escaped or been released from fighting forces, programs for disarmament, demobilization, and reintegration (DDR) have been established to assist them in returning and reintegrating into their families and communities.

These DDR programs represent a significant challenge in providing former child soldiers the special care and support needed while trying to reintegrate into society. Although it is widely accepted that children who have been illegally recruited by fighting forces should be treated as victims, they have in many cases been charged and detained as war criminals. In other situations, thousands of former child soldiers— especially girls—are afraid of being stigmatized by members of their communities and, therefore, do not register for DDR programs. Even when children do register for DDR programs, lack of funding, poor planning, and mismanagement often undermine the long-term psychosocial support, vocational training, and education these children need to successfully return to civilian life. And so, while some progress has been made in helping child soldiers, much more needs to be done, particularly with regard to preventing child involvement in the first place. According to the "Child Soldiers Global Report 2008" from the Coalition to Stop the Use of Child Soldiers:

> The overall picture is one of armed groups that have ignored international law and standards, that renege on commitments, are resistant to pressure and persuasion, or have so far proved to be beyond the reach of efforts to end the involvement of children in conflict and political violence.

According to the United Nations Convention on the Rights of the Child, every child has the right to survival; the right to develop to the fullest; the right to be protected from harmful influences, abuse, and exploitation; and the right to participate in family, culture, and social life. As soldiers, children are denied these rights. They are robbed of their childhood and exposed to terrible danger and to psychological, emotional, and physical suffering. The authors in *At Issue: Do Children Have Rights?* discuss other legal, ethical, developmental, and emotional issues concerning the rights children do or do not have.

1

Children Do Have Rights

United Nations Children's Fund (UNICEF)

The United Nations Children's Fund (UNICEF) is a multinational organization that provides health care, clean water, improved nutrition, and education to millions of children worldwide.

On November 20, 1989, world leaders came together in the United Nations General Assembly to adopt the Convention on the Rights of the Child. As the most-ratified human rights treaty in history, the convention articulates that children have the right to survive and develop; to be protected from violence, abuse, and exploitation; and for their views to be respected. It should be especially noted that children have the right to participate in decisions that affect their lives; this principle is less understood and championed than the basic rights of survival and protection. Experts, policy makers, and youth organizations are becoming increasingly aware that involving young people in decision-making processes enhances their development, resilience, and ability to protect themselves from abuse and exploitation.

On 20 November 2009, the global community celebrates the 20th anniversary of the adoption by the United Nations General Assembly of the Convention on the Rights of the Child. This unique document outlines universal standards for the care, treatment and protection of all individuals below age 18. It is the most widely endorsed human rights treaty in history, currently ratified by 193 States parties.

During the past two decades, the Convention has transformed the way children are viewed and treated throughout the world. It has exerted a pervasive and profound influence on national and international legislation, policy and programmes, public and private institutions, families, communities and individuals. And it has supported marked advances in survival, development, protection and participation across the world.

Despite the numerous challenges that remain in realizing children's rights, the Convention offers a vision of a world in which all children survive and develop, and are protected, respected and encouraged to participate in the decisions that affect them. This vision promotes a world of peace, tolerance, equity, respect for human rights and shared responsibility—in short, a world fit for children.

It is imperative to protect childhood as a period that is separate from adulthood.

The Convention on the Rights of the Child

The Convention on the Rights of the Child (henceforth referred to as 'the Convention') was adopted by the UN General Assembly on 20 November 1989 and entered into force on 2 September 1990. It is the most comprehensive human rights treaty and legal instrument for the promotion and protection of children's rights. Although there are provisions protecting child rights in other international human rights instruments, the Convention is the first to articulate the entire complement of rights relevant to children—economic, social, cultural, civil and political. It was also the first international instrument to explicitly recognize children as social actors and active holders of their own rights.

Under the provisions of the treaty, States parties are legally obliged to fulfil the rights of every child. The Convention comprises 54 articles and is based on four core principles: non-discrimination; best interests of the child; the right to life, survival and development; and respect for the views of children. Its broad scope and the importance it places on the agency of the child make it timelessly relevant to all actions that intend to promote, protect and fulfil children's rights.

The Convention is a powerful addition to the international human rights framework. Although it has been in existence for only two decades, it has achieved near-universal acceptance, having been ratified by 193 countries by 2009, with only two outstanding: Somalia and the United States, both of which have indicated their support by signing the treaty. The influence of the Convention and its Optional Protocols is already pervasive across continents and regions, countries and communities, and it will clearly remain the children's Magna Carta for decades—possibly even centuries—to come.

The Convention has significantly reaffirmed and enriched human rights. It reaffirms by applying many of the core principles of earlier international human rights instruments, such as universality and non-discrimination, directly to children. It enriches by consolidating and amplifying the provisions that are included in other human rights instruments, specifying the responsibilities and duties of States parties towards children. It incorporates rights for children that were not widely articulated—notably the right to participation—and stipulates that the best interests of the child should be a primary consideration in all actions towards them. It stresses that accountability for child rights lies with the duty bearers, including States parties, families and guardians, who are entrusted with ensuring that children's rights are realized.

"Terms of Childhood"

The full significance of the Convention extends well beyond its legislative implications. It has also helped transform attitudes towards childhood. In effect, the Convention has set the *terms of childhood,* outlining the minimum standards for the treatment, care, survival, development, protection and participation that are due every individual under age 18. Its articles reinforce a common understanding among societies that to fulfil the rights of children it is imperative to protect childhood as a period that is separate from adulthood, to define a time in which children can grow, learn, play and develop.

Under the Convention, children are rights holders rather than objects of charity. Fulfilling these rights is no longer an option for States parties but an obligation that governments have pledged to meet. Equally important is the optimism, clarity and steadfastness that the Convention captures for the future—that one day all children will enjoy a childhood with full respect for their rights, their basic needs provided for, protected from violence, abuse, exploitation, neglect and discrimination, and empowered to participate meaningfully in all decisions that affect their lives.

In its preamble and throughout its articles the Convention underscores the fundamental role of the family in the growth and well-being of children, recognizing the crucial importance of a loving, harmonious and understanding family environment for the full development of children. It obliges States parties to provide the family with all the means necessary to realize its responsibilities. . . .

The Right to Be Heard

Participation is one of the guiding principles of the Convention on the Rights of the Child, yet it is arguably taken less seriously than the other key principles of universality, the best interests of the child, and survival and development. To some extent, child participation may be seen as more controversial, challenging or difficult to implement than measures supporting child survival, development and protection because it is based on presenting children as rights holders rather than as recipients of charity. Also, there is less experience in this area among the child rights community than in survival, development and protection.

The Convention does not use the term 'participation' or explicitly state that children have a right to participate—except as a goal for children with disabilities (article 23). But it requires that their views be heard in relation to all matters that affect them and that their views be given due weight in accordance with their age and maturity (article 12). This right is part of a broader body of participation rights that children hold, starting with the right to freedom of expression (article 13), thought, conscience and religion (14), association (15), the right to privacy (16) and access to appropriate information (17) that provides the basis for the child's right to participate. The Convention refers to children's "evolving capacity" for decision-making—a revolutionary concept in international law—and this has profoundly influenced the practice of organizations working in the field during the past 20 years.

The right of children to participate is a fundamental component of respecting them as holders of their own rights. Being able to influence decisions that affect an individual is one of the defining characteristics of human rights principles. When it comes to designing opportunities for children to participate, conditions need to be adjusted in accordance with a child's age and maturity. They should not be pressured, constrained or influenced in ways that might prevent them from freely expressing their opinions or leave them feeling manipulated. Effective and meaningful participation depends on many factors, including the child's developing capabilities, the openness of parents and other adults to dialogue, and safe spaces within the family, community and society that allow such dialogue. It also depends on stakeholders being willing to take children's views into consideration. Much of the practice of child participation is based on children's right to expression in all matters affecting them—this has, to an increasing extent, guided legal processes in decisions relating to custody following divorce or disputes between parents and authorities over children taken into care.

The vast majority of public decisions affecting children are made, however, without considering the views of or involving children. Policies have traditionally focused on welfare, perceiving children as passive recipients of care and services, not public actors. In general, children are rarely able to exercise any influence over the resources allocated in their name. Much of the work of government and civil society is carried out without explicit recognition of children and young people. Interventions are implemented on behalf of children rather than with them.

Children are not generally seen as social and political actors. In most countries, individuals do not vote in national and local elections until they reach age 18. Children, therefore, often have no formal place at the decision-making table, and adult-controlled mechanisms are likely to be required for children's opinions to be represented. Children involved in political processes are often considered as technical actors who can provide useful information, rather than as citizens or political actors with rights to uphold and interests to defend.

Participation fosters the resilience of children and adolescents.

At conferences, adults may listen to children, but when it comes to the important decisions, children are often excluded. Youth parliaments may be little more than debating clubs where children learn about governance and politics. Some attempts at involving young people, moreover, are tokenistic—done more for the image of the adult organization bringing them together than for the benefit of the children themselves.

Participation and Empowerment

Children's participation has a vital role in empowering them in their own development. Through participation, girls and boys can learn vital life-skills and knowledge and take action to prevent and address abuse and exploitation. Participation initiatives are strengthened when children know and understand their rights. Consulting with children is critical to ensure that child survival, development and protection measures are adequate and appropriate.

There have been a growing number of initiatives in child participation since the Convention came into force in 1990. One highlight was the 2002 UN General Assembly Special Session on Children, an event that actively encouraged the participation of children in the principal decision-making body of the United Nations. More than 400 children from [more than] 150 countries took part in the three-day Children's Forum that culminated in a common statement from the participants reflecting their views.

The 2006 UN Secretary-General's Study on Violence against Children was the first United Nations study to consult with children and reflect and incorporate their views and recommendations. Children and adolescents participated in national, regional and international consultations, together with policymakers. To disseminate the findings of the study, child-friendly versions were created for a range of age groups. Children and adolescents were also strongly represented at the November 2008 Third World Congress against the Sexual Exploitation of Children and Adolescents in Rio de Janeiro (Brazil). . . .

In addition, child rights advocates are coming to recognize that participation by children and adolescents can play a vital part in protecting them from abuse, violence and exploitation. Participation fosters the resilience of children and adolescents and can enable them to become agents of change and to resist the processes that result in their abuse. It can also help them recover if they are abused, not least through sharing their experiences with their peers.

The theory and practice of children's participation is still in its infancy. But it has advanced significantly during the two decades since the Convention was adopted by the Member States of the United Nations. Moreover, the Convention has been a guiding force in encouraging greater child participation. Policymakers are becoming increasingly appreciative that involving young people in decision-making not only enhances children's development, protection and understanding of democracy, it improves outcomes for all. More children and young people are developing their capacity to participate and collaborate through youth organizations and networks to advocate for their rights.

2

Children's Rights Are Too Far Reaching

Patrick F. Fagan, William L. Saunders, and Michael A. Fragoso

Patrick F. Fagan is senior fellow and director of the Center for Research on Marriage and Religion at the Family Research Council (FRC), a Christian organization that promotes the traditional family unit. William L. Saunders is senior fellow and human rights counsel at the FRC. Michael A. Fragoso is a research assistant at the FRC.

The United Nations Convention on the Rights of the Child actually undermines the essence of family and parenthood by restricting the ability of parents to make decisions regarding how they parent their children. For example, United Nations committees urge children to challenge their parents in court regarding such time-honored parental responsibilities as supervision, discipline, moral and sexuality education, and even oversight of medical treatment. Most cultures and religions have respected the rights of parents to provide moral guidance for their children. The U.N. Committee on the Rights of the Child should not undermine parents' authority.

If the U.N. [United Nations] committees have their way, the freedom of parents to raise their own children, to shape their behaviors, and to safeguard their moral upbringing will be a relic of past centuries. That almost all cultures and religions have protected the time-honored role of parents in forming the character of children does not deter the U.N. from seeking changes in domestic laws to bypass parents on matters dealing with their children.

The U.N. Committee report to Belize recommends that the government set up legal mechanisms to help children challenge their parents.

The U.N. committees are urging states to give minor children:

- The right to privacy, even in the household;

- The right to professional counseling without parental consent or guidance;

- The full right to abortion and contraceptives, even when that would violate the parents' ethics and desires;

- The right to full freedom of expression at home and in school;

- The legal mechanisms to challenge in court their parents' authority in the home.

For example, the U.N. Committee on the Rights of the Child [CRC] recommends to the Japanese government that it "guarantee the child's right to privacy, especially in the family." Such a measure would establish legal and structural wedges between parents and their children in the home. Normally, when children rebel against their parents, society frowns. Yet the U.N. is attempting to put in place, in policy and law, structures that foster this type of rebellion.

Incites Children to Challenge Parental Role

Among the broad "rights" of children articulated in the CRC are freedom of expression; freedom to receive and impart all information and ideas, either orally, in writing, or in print, in the form of art, or through any other media of the child's choice; freedom of association; and freedom of peaceful assembly. This language could be interpreted to prohibit parents from legitimately limiting the associations and actions of their children, which can already be fraught with legal difficulties. Once these "rights" are embedded in domestic law, children could gain access to legal help from NGOs [nongovernmental organizations] or government agencies to challenge their parents in court.

Indeed, the U.N. committee report to Belize recommends that the government set up legal mechanisms to help children challenge their parents, including making an "independent child-friendly mechanism" accessible to children "to deal with complaints of violations of their rights and to provide remedies for such violations." In other words, the CRC committee is suggesting that the state create some entity *to supervise parents*, a structures that enables children in Belize to challenge their mother and father's parenting in court. Then the CRC committee goes even further: Its report asserts that it is "concerned that the law does not allow children, particularly adolescents, to seek medical or, legal counseling *without parental consent*, even when it is in the best interests of the child." This statement illustrates the committee's intent to undermine the authority of parents, especially those who hold traditional religious beliefs or who would disagree with the committee's radical interpretation of the CRC.

The U.N. committee's opposition to the freedom of parents to guide the moral education of their children is made clear in a rebuke directed at the United Kingdom in 1995. The committee stated that

> insufficient attention has been given to the right of the child to express his/her opinion, including in cases where parents in England and Wales have the possibility of withdrawing their children from parts of the sex education programs in

school. In this as in other decisions, including exclusion from school, the child is not systematically invited to express his/her opinion and those opinions may not be given due weight, as required under article 12 of the Convention.

The U.N. committee went even further in its recommendation to the Ethiopian government, urging it to change its laws so that "the limitation of the right to legal counsel of children be abolished as a matter of priority."

Consider the CRC committee's complaint to Austria: "Austrian Law and regulations do not provide a legal minimum age for medical counseling and treatment *without parental consent*." Austria, like all nations, has defined the age at which the child becomes legally independent of the parent. This effort by the U.N. committee to make states like Austria define a different age for medical counseling and treatment is targeted at removing parents' control over the moral formation of their children and the parameters of their children's sexual behavior.

The U.N. committee showed little awareness that Mali is among the poorest countries in the world, with 65 percent of its land area either desert or semi-desert. About 10 percent of the population is nomadic, and some 80 percent of the labor force is engaged in farming and fishing. Annual per capita GDP [gross domestic product] in Mali in 1998 was estimated to be $790. Yet the U.N. suggests that Mali allocate "adequate human and financial resources, to develop youth-friendly counseling, care and rehabilitation facilities for adolescents that would be *accessible without parental consent*, where this is in the best interests of the child."

Undermines Parental Influence Regarding Adolescent Sexual Behavior

The committee periodically issues "general comments" that are intended to flesh out the commitments inherent in the CRC treaty itself. The committee's General Comment No. 4

(2003) expounds upon "adolescent health and development in the context of the Convention on the Rights of the Child." This comment protects the right of children "to access appropriate information" regarding "family planning." It instructs states to allow minors to receive confidential medical care. They should have "access to appropriate information [regarding HIV/AIDS and STDs], regardless of their marital status and whether their parents or guardians consent." To that end the comment calls on states "to develop effective prevention programmes, including efforts aimed at changing cultural views about adolescents' need for contraception and STD [sexually transmitted disease] prevention and addressing cultural and other taboos surrounding adolescent sexuality." To that end, states should "take measures to remove all barriers hindering the access of adolescents to information, preventative measures such as condoms, and care." It goes on to urge states "to develop and implement programmes that provide access to sexual and reproductive health services, including family planning, contraception and safe abortion services where abortion is not against the law . . ."

The broader agenda will weaken the freedom and authority of parents to direct the moral education and attitudes of their children.

General Comment No. 4 also unilaterally expands the purview of the CRC's anti-discrimination clause (Article 2), which states that minors enjoy the rights of the treaty "without discrimination . . . with regard to 'race, colour, sex, language, religion, political or other opinion, national, ethnic or social origin, property, disability, birth or other status.'" The committee expands this list of protected classes to include "adolescents' sexual orientation." The established frameworks of anti-discrimination architecture in U.N. treaties lack sexual orientation as a protected class, as no binding U.N. treaty mentions "sexual orientation." Thus, for the committee to act as if it does is mere liberal activism.

Restricts Parental Ability to Discipline Children

CRC's interpretative committee is also embroiled in efforts to outlaw spanking by parents. The committee, in 2006, issued General Comment No. 8, "The right of the child to protection from corporal punishment and other cruel or degrading forms of punishment," which purports to clarify articles 19, 28, and 37 of CRC. The comment deals with *any* physical punishment, "however light," and makes no distinction between disciplinary spanking and serious physical abuse, ranging from whipping, to kicking, to biting (paragraph 11). As such, it calls for states to ban all physical punishment of children through criminal law—the object being for the law to treat spanking as it would the battery of an adult. Furthermore, the comment instructs countries to undertake vast educational campaigns to "raise awareness" about the right of children not to be spanked. State parties are required to submit data on their progress toward eliminating "corporal punishment" during their periodic reviews: "The Committee also encourages United Nations agencies, national human rights institutions, NGOs and other competent bodies to provide it with relevant information on the legal status and prevalence of corporal punishment and progress towards its elimination."

The United States is not a state party to CRC, and yet anti-spanking activists have used these pronouncements from the CRC committee to argue that "consensus is growing in the international community that physical punishment of children violates international human rights law. This principle of law is set forth in at least seven multilateral human rights treaties: the United Nations (U.N.) Convention on the Rights of the Child [being one of these] . . ."

Promotes Premarital Sex for Teenagers

The broader agenda is to seek changes in the laws of each nation that will weaken the freedom and authority of parents to direct the moral education and attitudes of their children. Nowhere is there a suggestion in the CRC recommendations to signatory nations that the role of parents should be strengthened. . . .

Contraception for teenagers is a highly controversial issue, especially when governments advocate access for minors over the wishes of parents. Nowhere in U.N. committee comments or on its website does the organization propose abstinence until marriage. Instead, U.N. committees repeatedly urge that teenagers have:

1. Universal access to contraceptives and abortions without their parents' permission, and

2. Access to medical counseling services without their parents' consent.

For example, the U.N. committee urged Ireland to "improve family planning services and the availability of contraception, including for teenagers and young adults." Yet, since making contraception available to single people three decades ago, Ireland has [experienced soaring] rates of divorce, out-of-wedlock birth, sexually transmitted disease, violence, and abortion. . . .

The U.N. committees give similar advice to other countries, including Peru, Russia, the Maldives, Yemen, and Macedonia. . . .

U.N. interpretative committees argue that restricting abortion, even for teenagers, is a form of subordination that violates human rights. But there is little reason to believe that U.N. representatives and bureaucrats know better than individual societies how they should shape their own cultures and laws on family, marriage, sexual behavior, and the raising and education of children.

3

Children Should Not Be Forced into Labor

David L. Parker

An occupational physician, photographer, and author, David L. Parker has written and photographed several books and has received the Christopher Award for work affirming the highest values of the human spirit.

Many nations have written laws and treaties—such as the Universal Declaration of Human Rights and the Convention on the Rights of the Child—to protect children from economic exploitation. Children continue to be forced into labor, however; statistics estimate that more than 320 million children under the age of sixteen are currently working worldwide. Because labor is so detrimental to a child's health, education, and safety, all nations must commit to regulating child labor and protecting their children.

Seeking to protect children from what are often deplorable working conditions, national and international communities have implemented laws and treaties to regulate child labor. Since the United Nations [UN] General Assembly adopted the Universal Declaration of Human Rights in 1948, dozens of international treaties concerning children's rights have been written.

The most encompassing of these is the UN's 1989 Convention on the Rights of the Child, which recognizes every

David L. Parker, *Before Their Time: The World of Child Labor*, New York: Quantuck Lane Press, 2007. Copyright © 2007 by David L. Parker. Reproduced by permission.

child's right to a primary school education. The convention also requires that nations protect children from economic exploitation "and from performing any work that is likely to be . . . harmful to the child's health or physical, mental, spiritual, moral or social development."

Any job, even one that does not seem harmful, can keep a child from attending school.

Another important treaty, the International Labour Office's Prohibition and Immediate Action for the Elimination of the Worst Forms of Child Labor, known as Convention 182, took effect in 1999. The International Labour Office (ILO), a branch of the United Nations, brings governments, workers, and employers together to promote safer and healthier working conditions. Convention 182 defines the worst forms of work as those associated with slavery and bondage, prostitution and pornography, illicit activities such as the drug trade, and other work that "is likely to harm the health, safety, or morals of children."

Labor Undermines a Child's Education

In spite of numerous laws and treaties, child labor remains an enormous problem, and millions of children lack access to basic education. Officially, more than 320 million children under age sixteen work worldwide and 25 percent of children do not complete a primary school education. In addition, almost 150 million children labor in the worst forms of work as defined by the ILO.

I have sometimes found it difficult to define when work is harmful, in part because of the importance of education in all children's lives. Any job, even one that does not seem harmful, can keep a child from attending school. Education provides a basis for a child's social, economic, and cultural development as well as the foundation for a healthy life. Children whose parents—particularly their mothers—are better educated are more likely to go to school and stay in school longer than children whose parents received little or no education. Further, children with less-educated mothers are more likely to work at an earlier age than children with educated mothers.

For many families, child labor is part of an intergenerational cycle of poverty, social exclusion, and lack of education. Poor families frequently lack the resources to ensure that their children go to school and stay healthy. An increased risk of illness contributes to the cycle of poverty. Young women who work and go to school or who work instead of attending school tend to have less-healthy children. A woman who has been to school for even a few years is more likely to marry later, obtain prenatal care, have a smaller family, and have healthier, better-educated children.

Even jobs that seem relatively safe place children at risk.

Child Labor Is Often Abusive

Another difficulty in understanding when work is harmful stems from the complexity or ambiguity of some job circumstances. For example, in 1993 and 1995 I photographed circus performers in Nepal and India. Although the children are often laughing and having fun, most are bonded laborers, a type of modern-day slave. Circus owners trick families into selling their children and then force them to work many years without pay. Neither the poor working conditions nor the slavery-like situation is obvious to a casual observer.

Other forms of work harm children in much more obvious and painful ways. In 2000, I photographed children at a rehabilitation center for young combatants in Sierra Leone. The children told stories of being drugged and forced to kill their parents or mutilate their neighbors. They also reported being shot during combat or beaten if they tried to escape from military service.

Some domestic workers are held in virtual slavery behind locked doors. Although I have photographs of children doing domestic chores—preparing food, caring for sisters and brothers, and washing clothes—only once did I gain access to a private home where children were employed. The employer did not allow me to take photographs.

Overall, working conditions for most children are pathetic. Many work sites lack sanitary facilities and clean drinking water. Child workers are exposed to excessive noise, clouds of dust, and other safety hazards. They eat food they find on the street or in the garbage dump, drink water and bathe in the same pond where they wash their tools and mix mud for making bricks, and live on the street or in cardboard huts.

Because children are still developing physically and mentally, harmful substances have a greater impact on them than on older workers. Pound for pound, children breathe more air, eat more food, and drink more water than adults do. Toxic chemicals such as mercury or lead can cause brain damage and permanent disabilities.

Children work long hours with little time for rest, play, or school, and even jobs that seem relatively safe place children at risk. Street vendors may leave for work at four or five A.M. and not return home until late at night. They go long stretches without eating. They may be robbed or abused. Street children often work for unscrupulous adults who refuse to pay them, cheat them of their earnings, or sexually exploit them.

Children who work face a wide array of dangers, from rats, wild dogs, and rotting wastes in garbage dumps and choking dust in stone quarries to injuries from high-speed machinery or the harsh chemicals used to tan leather. Some [child laborers] develop diseases typically associated with adults, such as arthritis or skin diseases. Most children do not wear protective equipment. Even when such equipment is provided, it does not serve children well since it is designed for adults.

I am encouraged by new data indicating that the number of working children around the world has declined over the past few years. Some nations have made strides to protect child workers from dangerous conditions, yet many others still fail to keep children safe, healthy, and educated. . . .

Agricultural work is fraught with hazards, including chemical pesticides.

Labor in Agriculture Is Particularly Harmful

More children work in agriculture than in any other industry. In some nations up to one third of agricultural workers are children. The popular image of a child on a farm is that of someone playing happily in a haystack. Most people wrongly assume that farmwork is healthy and that children who work on farms are part of a family business.

In reality, agricultural work is fraught with hazards, including chemical pesticides, large machinery, venomous insects and reptiles, unsafe drinking water, and parasitic diseases from contaminated irrigation water. Children on farms, plantations, and fisheries work long hours doing heavy, exhausting work. They plow fields with tractors or oxen, pick vegetables, cotton, fruits, and grains, and dive for shellfish. Children work in fields that have just been sprayed with pesticides. They work all day under the beating sun. Some labor as slaves on cocoa plantations.

During a recent trip to Nicaragua, I visited tobacco plantations. Children working in these fields are exposed to high levels of nicotine, which is absorbed through the skin and causes nausea and vomiting. The children also experience pesticide poisoning, with similar effects. Living conditions on plantations are poor: A dozen or more men, women, and children typically share a small room with no running water.

In many countries, large migrant communities follow the agricultural seasons from one region to another. In the United States, migrants may start the year in Texas and gradually work their way to the sugar beet fields in Minnesota's Red River Valley or the vegetable canning plants in southern Minnesota. In Turkey, entire communities move from the eastern part of the country to central Anatolia to pick cotton, dig potatoes, or harvest vegetables. Common to all migrant communities are low wages, unhealthy sanitary facilities, and meager opportunities for education.

Children in coastal areas fish or help farm coastal waters. In Indonesia, up to two thousand fishing platforms, called *jermals*, rise from stilts in the ocean around Java and Sumatra. Labor contractors lure young workers from inland villages with promises of good wages. Because the platforms lie far out at sea the children cannot escape. Platform workers subsist on rice; fresh fruit and vegetables are a rare luxury and potable water is brought in just once a week. The bosses often subject the children to physical and sexual abuse.

In eastern Morocco, children wander the desert tending sheep and herding camels. Similarly, in India and Nepal, children feed and herd camels and other animals. Many of these children work alone all day. Although this may be a traditional way of life for some, these children miss out on the opportunities afforded by even a basic education. . . .

For every child who is freed from forced labor and inhumane work, there are many more who continue to work. International and national laws have gone a long way in creating an awareness of child labor. However, it will take commitment on the part of all nations to eliminate the worst of its forms. This commitment must provide for the basic needs of children, families, and their communities. These needs include schools, food, books, and health care.

4

Sweatshops Benefit Children and Their Families

Nicholas D. Kristof

Nicholas D. Kristof is a regular columnist for the New York Times, *a two-time Pulitzer Prize winner for journalism, and co-author of the book* Half the Sky: Turning Oppression into Opportunity for Women Worldwide.

Americans have good intentions when they advocate for strict labor standards and boycotts of products made in sweatshops. But despite the long hours and meager pay, sweatshops actually raise living standards for many workers in poor countries and provide a means out of poverty. Without sweatshops, more people— many of them children—would be scavenging on the streets for longer hours, under worse conditions, and for even less pay. In the long run, the best way to help is to promote sweatshops and encourage importing their products.

Before Barack Obama and his team act on their talk about "labor standards," I'd like to offer them a tour of the vast garbage dump here in Phnom Penh.

This is a Dante-like vision of hell. It's a mountain of festering refuse, a half-hour hike across, emitting clouds of smoke from subterranean fires.

The miasma of toxic stink leaves you gasping, breezes batter you with filth, and even the rats look forlorn. Then the smoke parts and you come across a child ambling barefoot, searching for old plastic cups that recyclers will buy for five cents a pound. Many families actually live in shacks on this smoking garbage.

Sweatshops Are Better than the Alternative

Obama and the Democrats who favor labor standards in trade agreements mean well, for they intend to fight back at oppressive sweatshops abroad. But while it shocks Americans to hear it, the central challenge in the poorest countries is not that sweatshops exploit too many people, but that they don't exploit enough.

Talk to these families in the dump, and a job in a sweatshop is a cherished dream, an escalator out of poverty, the kind of gauzy if probably unrealistic ambition that parents everywhere often have for their children.

"I'd love to get a job in a factory," said Pim Srey Rath, a 19-year-old woman scavenging for plastic. "At least that work is in the shade. Here is where it's hot."

Another woman, Vath Sam Oeun, hopes her 10-year-old boy, scavenging beside her, grows up to get a factory job, partly because she has seen other children run over by garbage trucks. Her boy has never been to a doctor or a dentist, and last bathed when he was 2, so a sweatshop job by comparison would be far more pleasant and less dangerous.

I'm glad that many Americans are repulsed by the idea of importing products made by barely paid, barely legal workers in dangerous factories. Yet sweatshops are only a symptom of poverty, not a cause, and banning them closes off one route out of poverty. At a time of tremendous economic distress and protectionist pressures, there's a special danger that tighter labor standards will be used as an excuse to curb trade.

When I defend sweatshops, people always ask me: But would you want to work in a sweatshop? No, of course not.

But I would want even less to pull a rickshaw. In the hierarchy of jobs in poor countries, sweltering at a sewing machine isn't the bottom.

Sweatshops can help people.

Sweatshops Raise Living Standards

My views on sweatshops are shaped by years [of] living in East Asia, watching as living standards soared—including those in my wife's ancestral village in southern China—because of sweatshop jobs.

Manufacturing is one sector that can provide millions of jobs. Yet sweatshops usually go not to the poorest nations but to better-off countries with more reliable electricity and ports.

I often hear the argument: Labor standards can improve wages and working conditions, without greatly affecting the eventual retail cost of goods. That's true. But labor standards and "living wages" have a larger impact on production costs that companies are always trying to pare. The result is to push companies to operate more capital-intensive factories in better-off nations like Malaysia, rather than labor-intensive factories in poorer countries like Ghana or Cambodia.

Cambodia has, in fact, pursued an interesting experiment by working with factories to establish decent labor standards and wages. It's a worthwhile idea, but one result of paying above-market wages is that those in charge of hiring often demand bribes—sometimes a month's salary—in exchange for a job.

In addition, these standards add to production costs, so some factories have closed because of the global economic crisis and the difficulty of competing internationally.

A Factory Is a Good Thing

The best way to help people in the poorest countries isn't to campaign against sweatshops but to promote manufacturing there. One of the best things America could do for Africa would be to strengthen our program to encourage African imports, called AGOA [African Growth and Opportunity Act], and nudge Europe to match it.

Among people who work in development, many strongly believe (but few dare say very loudly) that one of the best hopes for the poorest countries would be to build their manufacturing industries. But global campaigns against sweatshops make that less likely.

Look, I know that Americans have a hard time accepting that sweatshops can help people. But take it from 13-year-old Neuo Chanthou, who earns a bit less than $1 a day scavenging in the dump. She's wearing a "Playboy" shirt and hat that she found amid the filth, and she worries about her sister, who lost part of her hand when a garbage truck ran over her.

"It's dirty, hot and smelly here," she said wistfully. "A factory is better."

5

Girls Have Fewer Rights and Opportunities than Boys

Una Murray and Patrick Quinn

The people who work for the International Labour Organization (ILO), a specialized agency of the United Nations, make up the International Labour Office. Its aims are to advance opportunities for women and men so they can obtain decent and productive work in conditions of freedom, equity, security, and human dignity. Una Murray is a consultant for the IPEC (International Programme on the Elimination of Child Labour) and Patrick Quinn is from the Geneva, Switzerland, office of the IPEC.

In most countries throughout the world, boys are afforded more rights and opportunities than girls, often because cultures and societies have passed down from generation to generation the belief that males are more important and valuable than females. As a result, especially in poor countries where child labor is an economic necessity for many families, girls are more likely to be denied an education and forced into labor, thus limiting any chance of their own to rise out of poverty. When governments and policy makers assess and implement strategies in response to the global economic crisis, special attention should be given to the discrimination against girls and the risks they face as a result of that discrimination.

In many countries and cultures the opportunities enjoyed by boys and girls differ, from the earliest stages of life through childhood and into adulthood. In fact, there are very few countries, societies or communities where girls have exactly the same opportunities as boys.

Access to education is a human right, and an important foundation for an individual's future prosperity and welfare. Yet in much of the world boys and girls continue to be treated differently in terms of access to education. Parents often place more value on their sons' education than on their daughters', and girls therefore are often taken out of school at an earlier age than boys. The result of these inequalities in education can be seen in global literacy statistics. Of the 16 per cent of the world's population who are unable to read or write a simple statement, almost two out of three are women.

The role of females is often viewed as being of less importance or value than that of males.

The discrimination against girls in education often stems from the view that in later life boys will have better labour market opportunities, while girls will assume domestic responsibilities, marry and move to another family. The inequalities in access to education mean that by the time girls reach the minimum age of employment many are already at a social and economic disadvantage.

Male Work Roles Are Considered More Important

Children are taught from an early age to model themselves on their parents. In most societies different gender roles mean that boys and girls engage in different activities. For example, a person is not born with the ability to do needlework or cook but acquires such skills over time. In most cultures it is more likely that girls will be taught such "female skills" than boys.

The different patterns of work of males and females may vary from society to society, However, most boys and girls are eventually channelled into what are perceived as male or female work roles. Generally speaking, the role of females is often viewed as being of less importance or value than that of males. Girls are more likely to engage in types of work for which earnings are relatively low.

The opportunities that girls encounter early in life may well determine their chances later on. If girls lack basic education and engage in child labour at an early age they may be condemned to a future of poverty.

Much of the work undertaken by girls is less visible than that of boys. Sometimes [individuals] outside the family and close community may be altogether unaware of it. Typical examples are work on farms and in small-scale agriculture, domestic work and work in small home-based workshops.

The often hidden nature of domestic work has given rise to particular concerns. Girls engaged in domestic work are frequently reported as being treated poorly and sometimes being physically abused. Although some of these cases do become public, the fact that the work takes place within the confines of a private home means that abuse very often goes unseen and unreported.

This problem extends beyond domestic work. Girls working in many other situations also have little contact with others outside the immediate work environment, thus giving rise to concerns for their safety and welfare. Some of the worst forms of child labour may entail girls being deliberately hidden from the outside world. Girls trafficked for labour and prostitution, for instance, can sometimes be held as virtual prisoners.

All children involved in child labour are vulnerable. To begin with . . . chances are that they come from poor families. They often belong to a socially excluded community, such as an ethnic or indigenous group or a group with a subordinate station in the social hierarchy. They may live in rural areas where there are few facilities. All these factors create disadvantages which have an impact on boys and girls alike, but girls face additional challenges.

Many Girls Are Denied a Basic Education

In many societies, cultural norms and values place women in an inferior position, and this can result in girls being discriminated against in many ways. For example, girls and young women are more likely to lack basic education, which makes it more difficult for them to protect their rights. As girls enter the labour market, they may be directly discriminated against [by] being paid less than boys or being restricted to menial tasks.

Along with factors such as their relative lack of physical strength, the absence of protective legislation and a failure to enforce such laws that [do] exist, the particular vulnerability of girls may also derive from the work situation itself. A United Nations report on violence against children drew attention to the problem of violence against children at the workplace, including both verbal and physical abuse. The report identified a number of sectors in which violence can be a particular problem. Most of these were sectors in which girls work in large numbers. The report also indicated that incidents of violence against under-age workers are unlikely to be reported.

The term "double burden" is used to describe the workload of those who are not only engaged in an economic activity but also have responsibility for unpaid domestic work in their own household. Women and girls often spend significantly more time on household chores and caring duties, such as child-rearing or attending to the sick, than do their male counterparts. The obligation to undertake household chores inevitably limits the time available for education and other activities.

It is commonly assumed that in many countries, as young people start working, the boys go into paid or unpaid economic activity while the girls engage in domestic work in the home. In practice, however, as shall be seen later in this report, the picture is more complex. It appears in fact that during childhood years, girls are employed in economic activities almost as much as boys, but in addition they are expected to devote significantly more time than boys to domestic duties. . . .

A vicious circle connects poverty, lack of education and child labour. The children of the poor who become child workers are themselves likely to be poor as adults, and their children in turn will face limited access to education and may also end up in child labour.

Research shows that educating girls is one of the most effective ways of tackling poverty. Educated girls are more likely to earn more as adults, marry later in life, have fewer and healthier children, and have decision-making power within the household. Educated mothers are also more likely to ensure that their own children are educated, thereby helping to avoid future child labour. Tackling child labour among girls and ensuring their right to education are therefore important elements of broader strategies to promote development.

In addition to the economic benefits of an educated female labour force, there are major social gains to be had from investing in the education of girls. These social benefits accrue to the individuals themselves, to their families and to society at large, and are sustained over time. . . .

Girls entering the labour force may be unclear about their rights.

Girls Are Treated Unequally in the Labor Market

For young persons, especially those suffering from poor education or poverty, the transition to the labour market can be particularly difficult. If they are unable to continue in education, by the time they reach the minimum age of employment, girls may already be at a disadvantage compared to boys.

Adolescent girls receive a variety of conflicting and confusing messages on their gender role from their parents, teachers, peers and the media, and these can often be decisive in channelling girls into working at home or taking up some form of employment outside the home. Such decisions may well affect their future capacity to support themselves and other household members.

Girls entering the labour force may be unclear about their rights and responsibilities on issues such as recruitment processes, wage systems, hours of work and other working conditions.

Vocational training and skills development for young men and women can play an important role in the transition to work, but opportunities for training are often limited. In many cultures the training that is available to young women is still restricted to traditional "female" skills. Many of the courses that are organized for young women actually reinforce their traditional roles and responsibilities (for example, health, beauty and child-care courses). Such an emphasis reduces the chances of their entering careers or fields that are perceived as "unfeminine." Young women who may have the opportunity to move beyond traditional skills and into newer or non-traditional occupations can become more "employable" and possibly earn a better living too.

Social factors often put pressure on women to engage in training that gives them access only to low-productivity and low-paid jobs. Sometimes young women require much encouragement and strong incentives to sign up for courses which they may have been told are not appropriate for them. Moreover, because many young women may already be mothers or have caring responsibilities outside work, logistical arrangements must be carefully planned.

Informal or "traditional" apprenticeships are a major source of skills and training for work. However, traditional apprenticeships tend to benefit boys more than girls. Girls may be told that certain occupations are [appropriate only] for boys, and employers of apprentices may restrict their choice of apprentices to boys. Encouraging girls to undertake apprenticeships can assist them in moving into "nontraditional" areas of work in which earnings may be better.

Information about training and employment opportunities sometimes does not reach young women. This may be because information is conveyed through channels that are inaccessible to them, or because placement services are geared to a male clientele. Much recruitment is through informal contacts and networks, and if young women are excluded from them they will not receive information.

Investment in the education and training of girls can play a very important role in helping to break the poverty cycle.

Many young women in the developing world have little choice but to get married early. Most young brides become young mothers. Apart from the health implications of early pregnancy, this restricts the access of young women to productive jobs. For young mothers, childcare and household chores tend to severely limit the possibility of further training or education. . . .

The Capability of Girls Is Undervalued

Girls and boys in situations of poverty are much more likely to be engaged in child labour than [youngsters] from more affluent families. Development policies that seek to reduce poverty and vulnerability of children are the key to achieving major and sustainable progress in tackling child labour. National poverty reduction strategies play an important role in determining the path of economic and social development in many developing countries, and it is important that issues of tackling child labour and promoting decent work for adults are integrated into such strategies.

Investment in the education and training of girls can play a very important role in helping to break the poverty cycle and should be a priority reflected in development plans and programmes. It is also important that plans and programmes address issues of gender inequalities in labour markets, which can limit the opportunities available to girls who have reached the minimum age of employment.

Social protection measures that target poor families can play an important role. Cash transfer programmes provide examples of resources being used to target and support vulnerable families, improving children's prospects of education and health care. Incentives such as school food programmes, which ensure that poor children receive a meal each day at school, can make the difference between a child being in school or in child labour.

The need to tackle child labour cuts across the mandate of many ministries. Ministries including those responsible for labour, education, finance, social affairs, women, children and youth should all have an interest in tackling child labour. Each should identify how [its] policies and programmes can be developed in order to support efforts to eliminate child labour and should give specific consideration to the situation of girls.

The provision of free, compulsory and quality education, at least up to the minimum age of employment, is the most important policy step a government can take to tackle child labour. Reducing the indirect cost of education (uniforms, books, transport, food, etc.) is also an important means of removing burdens that may otherwise prevent poor families from sending their children to school.

There are often specific barriers to girls' participation in education arising from cultural attitudes, safety concerns and the multiple disadvantages that girls may experience. Such barriers need to be identified at the national and local level so that appropriate strategies to tackle them can be identified and implemented.

Quality education requires a professional teaching force and a decent school environment. It is therefore important that national governments and donors support the education sector with adequate investment. There is a major worldwide shortage of teachers which needs to be tackled. Female teachers can serve as role models for girls and encourage their participation in education.

In developing education sector plans consideration must be given to those children who remain unreached by, or poorly served by, the education system. Children in child labour are a major part of this group. Available data and knowledge on child labour, including child labour among girls, can be used to support the targeting of children currently excluded from education. Good practices in tackling child labour among girls and promoting their education should be identified and scaled up into national initiatives. . . .

To support further policy and programme development, the knowledge base relating to the work of girls needs to be strengthened. This should include an in-depth analysis of the various aspects of child labour among girls, as well as of the relationship between child labour and the challenges facing adolescent girls in the labour market.

The global financial and economic crisis is pushing an increasing number of families into poverty. This could have a negative impact on child labour if families pull children out of school. When a poor family has to choose between sending either a boy or girl to school, in cultures in which a higher value is placed on boys education, girls are at particular risk of being pulled out of school.

Governments should ensure that measures implemented in response to the crisis do not have the effect of making the child labour situation worse. It is important that policy makers undertake an assessment of the possible employment, education and welfare implications of proposed recovery packages. The response to the crisis must include giving priority to budget expenditure that benefits poor and vulnerable households. Care must be taken to guard against the risk of both girls and boys being pulled out of school, and it should be noted that girls could be at special risk.

6

Female Genital Mutilation Violates Girls' Rights

Amnesty International USA

Founded in 1961 and the recipient of the Nobel Peace Prize, Amnesty International seeks to protect people wherever justice, freedom, truth, and dignity are denied. Through the organization's education, research, and action, governments have been persuaded to stop human rights violations.

Female Genital Mutilation/Cutting (FGM/C) is the removal of all or part of the female genitalia and subjects girls to excruciating pain, shock, infection, possible infertility, and sometimes even death. Predominantly practiced in twenty-eight North African countries, FGM/C is a traditional ritual that signifies the acceptance of a woman into society and her eligibility for marriage; it is rooted in a culture that aims to control women's sexuality and autonomy. Because the procedure clearly violates several basic human rights of girls, including the right to protection, health, gender equality, and physical integrity, many international treaties and conventions call for a worldwide strategy to end female genital mutilation.

I was genitally mutilated at the age of ten. When the operation began, I put up a big fight. The pain was terrible and unbearable . . . I was badly cut and lost blood . . . I was genitally mutilated with a blunt penknife. After the operation, no one was allowed to aid me to walk. . . . Sometimes I had to force myself not to urinate for fear of the terrible

Amnesty International USA, "Female Genital Mutilation/Cutting," February 2009. Reproduced by permission.

pain. I was not given any anesthetic in the operation to reduce my pain, nor any antibiotics to fight against infection. Afterwards, I hemorrhaged and became anemic. This was attributed to witchcraft. I suffered for a long time from acute vaginal infections.

—Hannah Koroma, Sierra Leone

What Is Female Genital Mutilation/Cutting?

Female genital mutilation (FGM/C) is the removal of part, or all, of the female genitalia. FGM/C may refer to clitoridectomy (removal of the clitoris), excision (removal of the labia minora), or infibulation (removal of the clitoris, labia minora and majora, and stitching together).

FGM/C is a dangerous procedure that often results in dire physical, sexual, and mental consequences. The procedure is usually performed in unsanitary conditions, using objects like broken glass, tin can lids, blunt knives, scissors, or razors. Victims are not given anesthesia or antibiotics and rarely have access to medical treatment. Infibulated women have their entire external genitalia cut, scraped, or burned out. The subsequent raw wound is stitched together with cat or lamb intestines or thorns, leaving a small opening for the passage of menstrual flow. The girl's legs are bound together for up to two months, immobilizing her while the wound heals over.

Conducting such a major procedure in poor hygenic conditions often results in infection, shock, hemorrhaging, abscesses, benign nerve tumors, cysts, excess scar tissue, progressively enlarging scars, and sterility. Because FGM/C is practiced as a group rite on many girls at once using the same cutting implement, it can easily cause the spread of HIV and other communicable diseases. Infibulation often causes a woman to retain urine and menstrual blood, leading to chronic urinary tract and pelvic infections that may cause sterility. Women must be continually cut open for childbirth and resewn afterward, a process which results in a mass of thick scar tissue.

This makes childbirth not only excruciatingly painful, but also extremely dangerous as it prolongs labor, obstructs the birth canal, and often causes perianal tears in the mother. Such ill effects of FGM/C are rarely blamed on the practitioner, but are instead blamed on witchcraft or the inadequate performance of rituals associated with the procedure.

FGM/C is rooted in a culture of discrimination against women.

More than 130 million girls have been subjected to female genital mutilation/cutting. The practice, most prevalent in Africa and some countries in the Middle East, is also prevalent among immigrant communities in Europe, North America and Australia.

Why Is FGM/C Practiced?

FGM/C is traditionally practiced as a ritual signifying the acceptance of a woman into society and establishes her eligibility for marriage. It is believed to inspire submissiveness in young women. Reasons given for FGM/C range from beliefs that touching the clitoris will kill a baby during childbirth, to hygenic reasons, to enhancing fertility and ensuring chastity.

In many societies, an important reason given for FGM/C is the belief that it reduces a woman's desire for sex, therefore reducing the chance of sex outside marriage. In FGM/C-practicing societies it is extremely difficult, if not impossible, for a woman to marry if she has not undergone mutilation. Marriage is often the only role available for women in FGM/C-practicing societies because they receive little education and are discouraged from pursuing a profession. In the case of infibulation, a woman is "sewn up" and "opened" only for her husband. Family honor is seen as dependent on a woman's sexuality. Therefore, restricting women's sexuality is believed to be vital.

FGM/C is rooted in a culture of discrimination against women. It is a human rights abuse that functions as an instrument for socializing girls into prescribed gender roles within the family and community. It is therefore intimately linked to the unequal position of women in the political, social, and economic structures of societies where it is practiced.

Every day, thousands of girls are targeted for mutilation.

Alternatively, women who do not undergo FGM/C in societies where it is the norm are often ostracized by their communities and are considered ineligible for marriage. In countries where females are not adequately educated and are unlikely to find employment, unmarried women are often forced to rely upon relatives and the community and are denied the means to support themselves. Because marriage is seen as the only significant and acceptable role for women in FGM/C-practicing societies—and only women who are mutilated are eligible to marry—FGM/C reasserts women's relegation to the domestic sphere, conferring upon women an inferior status and reducing them to mere child-bearers and objects of . . . male sexual fulfillment.

Is FGM/C a Human Rights Violation?

Every day, thousands of girls are targeted for mutilation. FGM/C involves the deliberate infliction of severe pain and suffering, and its effects can be life threatening. FGM/C is often perpetrated on girls from birth to adolescence and is a grave violation of children's human rights. Most survivors must face physical and mental scars for the rest of their lives. Violence against women and girls in the home or in the community is regarded as a "private" issue; the fact that perpetrators are private actors rather than state officials has often precluded FGM/C from being seen as a human-rights concern.

FGM/C is a manifestation of gender-based human-rights violations that exist in all cultures that aim to control women's sexuality and autonomy. Though striking because of its severity and scale, FGM/C cannot be viewed in isolation. Recognizing that FGM/C is one of many forms of social injustice that women suffer worldwide is key to creating societies in which women are valued as full and equal participants.

A human-rights perspective sets FGM/C in the context of women's social and economic powerlessness. Recognizing that civil, political, social, economic, and cultural rights are indivisible and interdependent is a crucial starting point for addressing the range of factors that perpetuate FGM/C. A human-rights framework affirms that the rights of women to physical and mental integrity, to freedom from discrimination, and to the highest standard of health are universal. Violations of these rights can never be justified.

General Recommendation No.19 of the UN Convention on the Elimination of All Forms of Discrimination Against Women (CEDAW) asserts, "gender-based violence . . . is . . . violence that is directed against a woman because she is a woman or affects women disproportionately. . . ." States are obligated under international law to prevent, investigate, and punish violence against women. Out of the twenty-eight African countries that practice FGM/C, twenty-six have ratified *CEDAW.*

The UN Declaration on the Elimination of Violence Against Women recognizes that violence against women not only deprives them of their civil and political rights, but also their social and economic rights[; the document states] that, "the underlying structural consequences of these forms of gender-based violence help to maintain women in their subordinate roles, contribute to their low level of participation and to their lower level of education, skills, and work opportunities." The Declaration provides that states should not invoke any custom, tradition, or religious consideration to avoid their obligation to eliminate violence against women, and that they must exhibit due diligence in investigating and imposing penalties for violence, and establishing effective protective measures.

How Can FGM/C Be Stopped?

Local NGOs [nongovernmental organizations] recognize that in order for legislation to be effective, it must be accompanied by a broad and inclusive strategy for community-based education and awareness raising. In addition to creating, upholding, and enforcing anti-FGM/C legislation, states have the obligation to target the underlying beliefs and inequality that perpetuate the practice and reinforce gender-based discrimination. NGO's therefore augment states' legislation by working to eradicate FGM/C by providing education, medical treatment, and advocacy to women in FGM/C-practicing communities.

Some local organizations have designed alternative rite-of-passage rituals similar to the traditional FGM/C ceremonies that replace genital mutilation with gift giving and celebration. Key to an effective approach is the exercise of cultural sensitivity when dealing with a custom that has been prevalent for many years and is thought of as normal and necessary by cultures that practice FGM/C.

Effective action requires an understanding of the complexity of perceptions and beliefs surrounding FGM/C. The cultural significance of FGM/C cannot be ignored. Eradicating the practice needs to be understood as a question not of eliminating rites of passage, but of redefining or replacing those rites in a way that promotes positive traditional values while removing the danger of physical and psychological harm.

FGM/C is a practice that compounds unspeakable violence against women and young girls with discrimination, repression, and inequality. As the issue becomes more visible in the public sphere, states that allow FGM/C to be perpetuated face increasing criticism and scrutiny by the international community. It must be made clear that no form of violence against women can be justified by any cultural claim.

7

Children Have the Right to Comprehensive Sex Education

Barbara Miner

Barbara Miner is a columnist for Rethinking Schools *magazine and writes frequently on social issues.*

Children have the right to sex education, which in turn helps fulfill other basic rights, including their need to information about matters that affect them and the right to have their needs met. Effective comprehensive sex education should contain information detailing sexual development and reproduction, methods of birth control, sexually transmitted diseases and HIV, abortion, and the different religious and cultural views on sex and sexual diversity. Armed with such information, young people are better equipped to make choices regarding their behavior.

For the last decade, schools around the country have been badgered and bribed into pumping ideas into students' heads through abstinence-only programs—that is, those relatively few schools that teach sex education in the first place. Beginning under former-president Bill Clinton and escalating under President George W. Bush, more than $1.5 billion in federal and state money has been poured into abstinence-only education. These programs, by law, have as their "exclusive purpose" teaching about the benefits of abstaining from sexual activity; prohibit schools from talking about contraceptives and condoms; and define healthy sexuality as "a mutually faithful monogamous relationship in the context of marriage."

Barbara Miner, "We're Here. We're Sexual. Get Used to It," *Colorlines*, May–June 2008. Reproduced by permission.

Problems with Abstinence-only Education

Over the past year, this surging abstinence-only education movement has finally shown signs of retreat. Numerous studies have proven it to be ineffective, even harmful, and a growing list of states have turned down federal money when it comes with abstinence strings attached. But as abstinence fades, the increasingly pressing question is this: What will rise in its place? Sex education in public schools has never been a resource priority and has rarely been described as forward thinking. So will the half-hearted sex education that preceded abstinence return in coming years? Will there be anything at all? Or are this country's policymakers prepared to embrace a comprehensive sex education that goes beyond fear tactics and acknowledges that sexuality is a normal part of life, even for teenagers?

Schools' failure to help students understand and embrace their sexuality has particular consequence for kids of color, who represent vast majorities in many public schools around the country. Sex and race have always formed a volatile brew in America. Racist stereotypes of hypersexual men and women compete with restrictive mores, coming from both inside and outside of communities of color, to circumscribe sexual expression. Too many young people are left to sort through this maelstrom with little or no guidance, and too many don't find their way. Blacks and Latinos account for 83 percent of teen HIV infections. Similar disparities exist with nearly every other type of sexually transmitted infection—Black girls are more than four times as likely to get gonorrhea as their peers, and syphilis is skyrocketing among Black teenage boys and slowly climbing among Latino boys. Late last year, federal health monitors announced that teen pregnancy went up in 2006 for the first time in 15 years. The largest spikes were found among Black and Native American girls.

"In essence, our country has viewed youth as hormonally driven accidents waiting to happen, so we give them sex ed that censors information," frets James Wagoner, head of the Washington, D.C. group Advocates for Youth. "We adults tell them not to have sex until they're married, and never mind that none of us ever followed that advice."

Not only are the [abstinence-only] programs ineffective, but in many cases give kids inaccurate information.

The Beginnings of Abstinence-only Education

While most associate abstinence-only education with the [President George W.] Bush administration, such policies go back to 1981, when Congress started funding so-called "chastity education." The Supreme Court ultimately curtailed the programs because of their close association with religious proselytizing, but conservatives didn't stop organizing.

In 1996, abstinence-only found new footing when then-president Clinton signed welfare legislation onto which conservative activists had tacked abstinence-only education funding. Before long, abstinence-only efforts dominated school sex ed, even though no research had established the curricula as scientifically sound. [George W.] Bush expanded the programs and ratcheted up annual funding for them and then exported the idea by tying abstinence to foreign aid for HIV/AIDS initiatives.

Last year, that tide turned. The movement had always been controversial, but in April 2007 it was severely wounded when a comprehensive report found that students in abstinence-only programs were just as likely to have sex. An October report by the Government Accountability Office added that not only are the programs ineffective, but in many cases they give kids inaccurate information. That study reinforced a previous one by California Democrat Rep. Henry Waxman, that found several federally funded abstinence-only curricula were not only giving students inaccurate information, but were also pushing gender stereotypes—one program listed "financial support" as a "major need" for women and "domestic support" as one for men. And still more bad news came in December: While pregnancy and birth rates for U.S. teenagers had been falling since about 1991, there was an unexpected jump of almost 4 percent in 2006, according to a report by the National Center for Health Statistics.

The cavalcade of bad press emboldened states already uncomfortable with the programs. As of this February, 16 states had said they would no longer take federal funds for abstinence-only programs, which mandate states to partially match the federal dollars.

But that hasn't stopped the abstinence-only movement, which has grown into a nationwide industry of hundreds of politically connected groups receiving public dollars to push their scientifically suspect information on public schools. In an era of budget shortfalls, a disturbing number of schools say "yes" when the groups offer their abstinence-only curriculum for free. And while the abstinence movement may be wounded, Wagoner of Advocates for Youth warns that it is far from defeated. Powerful Democrats in Congress such as Dave Obey, the chairman of the House Appropriations Committee, have shown little concern about changing the abstinence-only approach.

"Politicians, including Democrats like Obey, are hypocritical when they demand responsible behavior from youth and then shut off all access to the information—access and support that they need," Wagoner argues. "That's not morality—it's irresponsibility and rank hypocrisy."

And what has been President [George W.] Bush's response to the raft of information disputing the merits of abstinence-only education? His proposed 2009 budget calls for $204 million in abstinence-only funding, including an increase of $28 million for the largest program, which is distributed through community-based groups.

Comprehensive Sex Education

Paul Zettel is a health education teacher at Riverside University High School in Milwaukee, Wisconsin, where more than 60 percent of the students are African American, 17 percent are Latino, and 8 percent are Asian. Special education students account for more than 15 percent of the students; there's a sizable group of English language learners, and most of the students are from low-income families. In other words, Riverside is a typical urban public high school.

Zettel teaches sex ed as part of a semester-long health class for sophomores, and his primary goal is to teach students the skills needed to make healthy decisions about their emotional, physical, intellectual and sexual health. A comprehensive sex ed approach that talks about contraception is only the first step, Zettel emphasizes. His students need far-broader support in developing healthy sex lives than just information on preventing STIs.

The entire paradigm, given the expectations within a sexist society, has to be challenged.

"People don't understand that our youth at Riverside are living in multiple health crises," Zettel says. "More than 30 percent are clinically depressed; one out of every two has been sexually assaulted by age 16. More than 15,000 students in the Milwaukee schools have a parent in prison or in jail on any given day, and kids come into class grieving because a friend was shot, or an uncle died. These epidemics are weighing our children down."

Milwaukee is no stranger to social problems. It consistently ranks in the top three of cities with the highest percent of births to teens and the highest child poverty rates. And then there's the staggering level of sexual assault in both the city and state. Juveniles accounted for the majority of sexual assault victims in 2001; almost half of girls younger than 15 said their first intercourse was nonconsensual; and about half of teenager mothers were sexually molested before their first pregnancy, according to a report last year from United Way of Greater Milwaukee.

Limitations of All Sex Education

One of the limitations of almost all sex ed, whether comprehensive or abstinence-only, is that it is based on fear: do this or else you'll get a disease, be careful or else you'll get pregnant and your life will be ruined. But there's another, often unmentioned, problem. Young women are rarely given the skills they need to resist unwanted sexual advances, especially from older boyfriends. Few sex ed classes teach students— either young men or young women—how to understand the difference between flirting and harrasment, or that the right to say "yes" to sex must also include the right to say "no."

"The entire paradigm, given the expectations within a sexist society, has to be challenged," says Ellen Bravo, the Milwaukee-based former director of 9to5, National Association of Working Women, who has been involved in anti-sexual-harassment training for more than 20 years. "We need to challenge the double standard that men with a lot of sexual experience are cool [but] women with a lot of experience are sluts and whores. Being sexual beings does not mean women have to be pressured into giving sexual favors, but that they have the right to a sexual relationship among equals."

But whether a Milwaukee sex ed class may invite Bravo in to discuss these issues is a matter of chance. While district policy nominally calls for comprehensive sex education, what does or doesn't happen in a particular school varies wildly—a confounding reality in school districts around the country.

"Overall, sex education in Milwaukee is definitely on the back burner," notes Jennifer Morales, a school board member who has two teenage sons in the public schools. She cites a number of factors for the haphazard nature of sex ed in

Milwaukee's schools: the out-of-control emphasis on testing; the year-after-year budget cuts; and the impossibility of teaching all the various curriculum mandates, whether from the reds, the state or the district: "I don't see any motion one way or another, either for more or less comprehensive sex ed. We've decentralized to the point where nobody is responsible for moving it forward, and we're in a morass."

And like many school districts, educators have little incentive and every reason to avoid becoming trailblazers. "There's a very real fear of public backlash if we push too hard on sex ed issues," Morales says. "We're not at the point where we have accepted that teenagers are sexual beings, and if you talk about that too much it's a one-way ticket out of teaching."

8

Children Should Be Taught Sexual Abstinence

Valerie Huber

Valerie Huber is the executive director of Parents for Truth and the National Abstinence Education Association.

Abstinence-centered sex education provides extensive information for adolescents regarding healthy and unhealthy relationships, skills development for decision-making, and sexually transmitted disease (STD) and risk avoidance strategies. Whereas comprehensive-based sex education encourages activities that put teens at risk for STDs and pregnancy, research has shown that abstinence education delays sexual onset and reduces sexual activity.

So common are sex scandals in Washington [D.C.], it comes as no surprise that the mainstream media hardly took notice when the Centers for Disease Control [and Prevention] (CDC) revealed disturbing news about teen sex in its Youth Risk Behavior Surveillance System (YRBSS) data for 2007.

Since 2005, mere teens are having sex, with more partners. Rates are up for teen pregnancies. Fewer young people are using condoms. This information runs parallel to the shocking statistic, released earlier this year [2008], that one in four teen girls has at least one STD [sexually transmitted disease].

For parents and public health officials, the YRBSS data signals a warning. In spite of increased HIV/AIDS education and millions of taxpayer dollars spent in the name of "comprehensive" sex education, teens remain at risk for the dangers associated with casual sex. The sex-saturated culture that sends the message that teen sex is expected and without consequence is often reinforced in sex education classes across the country, and so it comes as no surprise that risky behaviors are on the uptick.

Comprehensive Sex Education Undermines Abstinence

According to the Guttmacher Institute, 68 percent of public schools teach so-called comprehensive sex education. According to the U.S Department of Health and Human Services, comprehensive sex education programs spend less than 10 percent of class time promoting the merits of abstinence but an inordinate amount of time marginalizing the risks of casual sex.

In a section called "How to Make Condoms Fun and Pleasurable," the *Be Proud, Be Responsible* guidebook, a CDC-approved comprehensive sex education manual, invites students as young as 13 to "brainstorm ways to increase spontaneity" by encouraging teens to "eroticize condom use with a partner" and gives tips [such as] "use more lubrication," "act sexy and sensual" or "think up [a] sexual fantasy using condoms." The same guidebook also lists activities like showering together and body rubbing as "green light" activities.

Techniques taught in this contraception-based curriculum and countless others like it are encouraging activities that put teens at risk for STDs and other negative consequences. The new YRBSS data reveal the fall-out. Contraceptive sex education does not provide practical skills for maintaining or regaining abstinence but instead arms teens with sometimes explicit information that promotes gateway-to-intercourse activities.

When there is a shift in risky youth behavior, critics are quick to blame abstinence-centered education. After all, it did receive $174 million in federal funding last year. Abstinence education is an easy scapegoat for those who are ideologically opposed to it, but it can't be ignored that comprehensive sex education programs, which have received funding for the past 25 years, still receive more than double the funding that is given to abstinence education.

Abstinence Education Is Thorough

It is time that taxpayers and parents receive an accounting for the proliferation of harmful contraceptive sex education programs in our schools. That is why NAEA [National Abstinence Education Association] recently launched its Parents for Truth Campaign (www.parentsfortruth.org). Youth should no longer reap the devastation caused by the dangerous messages of this failed public health approach. Teens deserve the risk avoidance strategies [detailed] in abstinence education.

Within an abstinence education program, teens receive all the information they need in order to make healthy choices.

Abstinence-centered education, as funded by Congress, is decidedly more inclusive than "just say no." The term, "abstinence only" is strategically attached to this funding by opponents to create the false perception that abstinence education is a narrow and unrealistic approach. Abstinence education is overwhelmingly more comprehensive and holistic than other approaches and focuses on the real-life struggles that teens face as they navigate through the difficult adolescent years.

Abstinence education realizes that "having sex" can potentially affect a lot more than the sex organs of teens, [and,] as research shows, can also have emotional, psychological, social, economic and educational consequences. That's why topics frequently discussed in an abstinence education class include how to identify a healthy relationship; how to avoid or get out of a dangerous, unhealthy, or abusive relationship; developing skills to make good decisions; setting goals for the future and taking realistic steps to reach them; understanding and avoiding STDs; information about contraceptives and their effectiveness against pregnancy and STDs; practical ways to avoid inappropriate sexual advances and why abstinence until marriage is optimal.

So, within an abstinence education program, teens receive all the information they need in order to make healthy choices. And all of these topics are taught within the context of why abstinence is the best choice.

Research shows that abstinence education delays sexual onset, helps sexually experienced teens discontinue their sexual activity, and helps currently sexual active teens reduce [their] number of partners while using condoms at the same rate as their peers.

As lawmakers begin to debate funding levels for the public health of American's youth, Congress will consider the YRBSS data. Lawmakers must recognize the growing body of research that affirms abstinence-centered education is effective, and they must honor the 80 percent of American parents who, despite political ideology, support continued funding for abstinence education.

9

Minors Should Have the Right to Consent to an Abortion

Caitlin Borgmann

Caitlin Borgmann is a professor at the City University of New York School of Law and is the editor of the Reproductive Rights Prof Blog.

On July 14, 2009, Illinois joined thirty-four other American states in mandating parental notification before a teenager can obtain an abortion despite evidence that such a restriction is irrational, often unnecessary, and sometimes harmful. At a time when most states recognize the rights of minors to choose their own sexual and reproductive health care, mental health services, and alcohol and drug abuse treatment, it should appear obvious that the ultimate goal of parental notification laws is not to involve parents but to eliminate abortion altogether. Teenage girls—especially ones who lack loving and supportive parents—should have the right to an abortion without parental consent. Their lives could be in danger without it.

On July 14 [2009], in *Zbaraz v. Madigan*, the Seventh Circuit lifted a permanent injunction that had prevented enforcement of Illinois' parental notice for abortion law since its enactment in 1995. The decision hinged on an arcane question of state procedural law, and the opinion did not break new legal ground on the abortion issue. What is noteworthy

Caitlin Borgmann, "Abortion Parental Notice Laws: Irrational, Unnecessary and Downright Dangerous," *Jurist*, July 27, 2009. Reproduced by permission.

about the decision, then, is precisely what for many might seem mundane: Illinois will now join the ranks of 34 other states in enforcing some kind of parental involvement requirement before a teenager can obtain an abortion. The court emphasized the unexceptional nature of its decision, noting that "[m]any, if not all of the concerns first raised against parental involvement laws in the 1970s and early 1980s have been addressed" in laws like Illinois'.

Teens who avoid telling their parents often have compelling reasons for doing so.

The Irrationality of Parental Involvement Laws

This soothing language, however, obscures the fact that a substantial majority of states blithely impose what are in reality irrational laws that impose appalling burdens on the teenagers who are least able to consult with their parents about their pregnancies. States continue to enforce these restrictions despite evidence that they do not serve their intended purpose . . . and are unnecessary for most teens and downright dangerous for others. It is worth a pause to reflect on these laws that now seem scarcely to merit a yawn from the courts.

On their face parental involvement laws appear intended to keep parents informed and to ensure minors' wellbeing. But let's remember that the main proponents of parental involvement laws oppose abortion altogether. Their ultimate goal is not to improve familial communication but to eliminate abortion as an option for all women. A strategy memo written by anti-abortion-rights movement leaders James Bopp, Jr., and Richard E. Coleson, for example, encourages the passage of "parental involvement" laws, among other "incremental" restrictions on abortion. They argue that such laws "keep the abortion issue alive and . . . also translate into more disfavor for all abortions, which in turn reduces abortions."

Parents understandably want to be involved in their minor children's important life decisions, but this desire has not translated to parental involvement requirements for other sensitive medical decisions that minors make. Most states recognize that mandating parental involvement for sensitive medical treatment will have the hazardous drawback of deterring many minors from seeking care at all. As the Guttmacher Institute reports, "The legal ability of minors to consent to a range of sensitive health care services—including sexual and reproductive health care, mental health services and alcohol and drug abuse treatment—has expanded dramatically over the past 30 years." Minors in most states can consent to services such as contraception, prenatal care, and treatment for sexually transmitted infection. In many states, minors can even relinquish their children for adoption and consent to medical care for their children. Parental involvement laws for abortion stand out as the glaring antithesis to this trend.

Studies have shown that most pregnant teens voluntarily involve their parents in their abortion decisions. Even in the absence of a parental involvement law, about six in ten teens consult at least one parent before seeking an abortion. Teens who avoid telling their parents often have compelling reasons for doing so. Teenagers may suffer abuse when their parents discover they are pregnant; other teens are thrown out of the house. Some parents actively prevent their children from obtaining an abortion. Some minors function as the *de facto* adult in dysfunctional homes where the custodial parent is largely absent. Because of the dangers that minors can confront when forced against their own judgment to involve their parents, most major medical groups, including the AMA [American Medical Association] and the American Academy of Pediatrics, oppose mandating parental involvement for abortion.

The Futility of the Judicial Bypass

The [U.S.] Supreme Court has held that teenage girls, like adult women, have a constitutional right to determine the fate of their pregnancy. Thus, while states can require parental consent or notice for abortion, the Court requires that they provide some alternative for teens who do not wish to consult their parents. The alternative that has become standard is the judicial bypass. The judicial bypass allows a teenager to seek permission from a court rather than involve her parents in her decision. Not surprisingly, this option holds many perils for a pregnant teenager. Teens must navigate the process of a court hearing. They must find the time, often during school hours, to appear in court before an imposing stranger to discuss this most intimate of issues. Although the Supreme Court has required that the process be confidential, in practice it can be difficult for teens to keep their presence secret. In small towns, they may know the court personnel. In one instance, a teen waiting in the hallway for her hearing encountered her sister's entire class, which had come to the courthouse on a field trip.

Ironically, properly functioning bypass systems demonstrate the irrationality of requiring court waivers in the first place. When bypass processes work as envisioned, the vast majorities of minors' petitions are granted. This is because the law requires that judges must grant a waiver of parental involvement if a minor is either mature enough to consent on her own or if an abortion without notice would be in her best interests. The vast majority of minors fall into one of these two categories. For example, one study in Massachusetts showed that out of 477 petitions, only one minor was denied a waiver. Indeed, a report by the AMA found that minors' decision making process on abortion is comparable to that of adults aged 22–25. Thus, when bypasses work correctly, they ensure nothing more than that minors needlessly parade through courtrooms in order to be granted the right to do what they can already do for a host of other sensitive medical treatments: provide their own consent.

On the other hand, bypass processes often don't work. Helena Silverstein's book, *Girls on the Stand: How Courts Fail Pregnant Minors*, documents the myriad ways in which the bypass process can fail. Court personnel are often misinformed about the procedures. Some judges ignore confidentiality requirements. Other judges, ideologically opposed to abortion, refuse to hear bypass petitions, or they conduct hearings but then lecture teens about their immorality and routinely deny waivers. In these all too frequent circumstances, the "bypass" becomes a roadblock. While minors facing such roadblocks can try to seek an abortion in another state, not all will be able to do so. As the Guttmacher Institute points out, "[t]o travel out of state, a minor must have access to transportation and must be within a reasonable distance of a state with less restrictive laws. The degree to which minors exercise this option varies by age, socio-economic status and access to public transportation."

The *Zbaraz* court conceded that the bypass process may be "intimidating" and may pose "practical problems" for many minors. However, the court demurred, "[W]e fail to see a better alternative." This is a cop-out. The court may have felt compelled to follow precedent, but it should not pretend that precedent dictated a good outcome. Healthcare providers should always strongly encourage teens to involve their parents in their abortion decisions. But laws like the one that will now be enforced in Illinois do nothing to help teenagers, while imposing traumatic hurdles, and sometimes grave danger, on those who lack loving and supportive parents to whom they can turn.

10

Middle School Students Should Have Access to Birth Control

Abigail Jones and Marissa Miley

Abigail Jones, a reporter and staff writer, cowrote the book Restless Virgins: Love, Sex, and Survival at a New England Prep School *with Marissa Miley. Marissa Miley's work has appeared in* Esquire *and* USA Today, *and she was the content writer for Harvard University's Initiative for Global Health.*

It is a fact: Boys and girls as young as age eleven are engaging in sexual activity. Facing up to that fact, school officials in Portland, Maine, decided to provide birth control and sexual counseling to their middle-school students. Many people are concerned about that decision, partly because they do not want to admit that their kids are having sex, and partly because they believe parents should be notified if their children receive birth control. Nevertheless, the Portland school officials made the right choice because now their students will be better equipped when making decisions about their sexual activity.

Congratulations, Portland, Maine, for voting to provide birth control and counseling about sexually transmitted diseases (STDs) to middle schoolers. You are no longer a victim of the generational chasm between adults and teenagers. You've admitted what so many deny: teens are sexually active, and we need to help them stay safe and make smart choices.

Abigail Jones and Marissa Miley, "On Providing Birth Control for Middle Schoolers," The Huffington Post, October 19, 2007. Reproduced by permission of the authors.

The Truth About Kids and Sex

No matter how innocent we want middle schoolers to be, the truth is that girls and boys aged 11, 12, 13, and 14 years are hooking up, performing oral sex, and having intercourse. Not everyone is, but even when a student chooses not to engage in these behaviors, his or her friends or classmates may be. To anyone who disagrees, here's a reality check:

"One [youth in eight is] sexually experienced, having engaged in intercourse, oral sex or both before the age of 14," the *Journal of Adolescent Health* reported in 2006. According to the Project Connect study, supported by the Centers for Disease Control and Prevention:

- "9 percent reported ever having sexual intercourse . . . and 8 percent ever had oral sex (active or receptive)."

- "Of those who reported intercourse, 36 percent were age 11 or younger at first sex, 27 percent were 12, 28 percent were 13, and 9 percent were 14 or older."

- "Alarmingly, 43 percent of sexually experienced participants reported multiple sex partners."

Note that more girls and boys had sex at age 11 than age 12, at age 13 than age 14. If this data doesn't convince you, here are a few more findings. These examples may not be about intercourse, but they illuminate the over-sexed landscape in which girls and boys are growing up today.

One of the girls in *Restless Virgins: Love, Sex, and Survival at a New England Prep School*, a nonfiction book about seven high school students, had her first sexual experience in sixth grade—with sex dice. One die listed body parts (neck, lips), and another listed actions (lick, suck); all she had to do was roll and follow the instructions.

Last October, Tesco, the U.K. [United Kingdom] mega store, was forced to pull a pole-dancing kit from the toys and games section of its Web site, frequented by moms, dads, and, most importantly, young girls and boys. The toy came in a pink plastic tube, had featured bubble letters and a Barbie-type character, and said, "Unleash the sex kitten inside."

And just recently, we heard that the latest bar mitzvah gift is a blowjob at the back of the bus on the way to the DJ [disc jockey] party.

It's all startling to us, too, and we're the ones who just spent over two years immersed in teenage life, listening to guys brag about their sexual conquests and girls convince themselves that they really did want to give that guy—who didn't call or like her enough—oral sex. But there's a difference between being startled and being in denial.

Providing birth control to sexually active middle schoolers is a crucial step.

The Choice Between Informing Parents and Protecting Children

Some opposing the Portland decision argue that 11-year-olds should not be given birth control without a parent's consent. It's a fuzzy line. Of course parents should be involved in their children's health care. Of course they should know whether . . . their sons and daughters are having sex. It's easy to tell adults to talk with teens about sex, but it's another thing to actually do it.

The generational chasm we mentioned above is very real and very wide. We get it: a mother may not want to admit that her 12-year-old daughter is having sex in her boyfriend's basement after school. But that mother needs to know this is going on. So what about girls and boys whose parents don't know—or don't want to face—their children's sex lives?

Thank goodness for Portland, Maine.

Providing birth control to sexually active middle schoolers is a crucial step. Condoms and the pill don't protect against

STDs, but [these measures] will prevent girls from getting pregnant and lower the risk of transmitting many diseases. Providing counseling is just as critical. As we discovered, teenagers know about STDs and condoms. They've had sex ed. They're familiar with the Rolodex [a compact office filing system] of ramifications, and younger girls and boys need to be, too. And what all of them need is education about the emotional consequences of their sexual behavior.

How will you feel after giving a guy, who's not your boyfriend or even your friend, oral sex?

Do you really want to hook up with those two guys, at the same time, while another friend watches? You do? Okay, why?

These are tough questions, but they're not asked enough, if at all. Girls and boys are coming of age in a culture that's saturated by sex. They're affected by this culture, and they need the tools to make the right decisions. This isn't about religion or moral judgment. This is about protecting young people who are already engaged in sexual behavior. Thankfully, girls and boys in Portland, Maine, will now have access to birth control and counseling, and therefore be more equipped to make smarter and safer decisions about their sexuality. It's time for other school districts to wake up and take notice.

11

Middle School Students Should Not Have Access to Birth Control

Amy Topolewski

Amy Topolewski, a 2009 graduate of the University of Michigan at Dearborn, studied journalism and health policy and was a staff columnist for the school newspaper, the Michigan Journal.

Because seventeen pregnancies were reported at middle schools in Portland, Maine, the city's school officials voted to make a full range of birth control available to their students, with or without parental knowledge. The problem is not that middle school students are getting pregnant, however; the problem is that these students—eleven- and twelve-year-olds—are having sex in the first place. Instead of encouraging children to engage in sexual activity by providing them with birth control, parents and teachers should provide counseling to prevent sexual activity from happening at all.

"Birth control is just offering protection. It is no different than giving out bike helmets or immunizations."

These are the disturbing words of one reader in response to reading a *USA Today* article about offering birth control pills to girls as young as 11. I hardly think that you can equate riding a bike with having sex, but especially not at the age of 11.

On Oct. 18 [2007], school officials in Portland, Maine voted to make birth control pills available to students at one of the city's middle schools. King Middle School will be Maine's first school to have a full range of contraception available, including birth control pills, patches and condoms. Condoms have been offered by the school since 2000.

> *Providing contraception to children this young is not getting at the root of the problem.*

Perhaps the condoms have been ineffective (or too big for the pre-pubescent bodies of 11- and 12-year-olds), because the decision to offer oral contraceptives to girls is based on 17 reported pregnancies at Portland's three middle schools in the last four years.

Not Confronting the Real Problem

If condoms have been available to students over the last four years and didn't prevent pregnancies, what makes school officials believe that birth control pills or patches will be any more effective in preventing pregnancy? If the availability of condoms didn't work, perhaps girls, who are said to mature faster than boys, will be responsible enough to remember to take the pill every day. No 11- or 12-year-old child, whether girl or boy, should be held responsible for weighing the consequences—emotional and physical—of having sex.

The truth of the matter is this: Providing contraception to children this young is not getting at the root of the problem. The problem is not that girls are becoming pregnant, though this is a horrifying reality. Rather, the problem is that 11-year-olds are having sex at all. This problem is being ignored. Instead of offering counseling to attend to the larger problems that are surely at work in the life of an 11-year-old who is having sex, school officials have found a way to treat only the symptoms.

Another problem with this decision is that treatment at the school's health center is confidential under state law. Though children would need to have their parents' permission to seek treatment at the clinic (which also treats the common cold or headaches), parents would not necessarily know if their child was prescribed birth control pills or given other forms of contraception. The only way parents would be aware is if their child came to them and told them.

The board's decision sends the message that having sex at this age is OK.

This decision is said to have been made largely because parents are not doing their jobs. Agreed. But this decision is just putting up another wall between parents and children by leaving parents out of the loop when it comes to the sexual activities of their children.

Encouraging Sexual Activity

The controversy over the decision [revolves] largely around the idea of whether . . . it encourages promiscuity among students. It is too soon to test the validity of this idea, but undoubtedly the availability of contraception magnifies the fact that there are indeed children as young as 11 or 12 having sex. It makes students who have not yet even given a thought to the opposite sex much more aware of the idea. At such a young and impressionable age, who's to say that this new awareness will not increase their curiosity concerning sex?

The availability of contraception may also provide students with a false sense of security. Though no form of birth control completely guards against pregnancy or STDs, children may get the idea that by using contraception, they are immune to any negative consequences of sex. The board's decision sends the message that having sex at this age is OK as long as protection is used. Ultimately, this decision is wrong.

During the 2006–2007 school year, five of 134 students who visited King's health center admitted having had sex, according to the lead nurse in the city's school health centers. So, instead of focusing on the 129 students who have not ventured down the road of sexual activity, the board has put all students at risk for the sake of five. It's not that these five students are insignificant. If anything, they, 11- and 12-year-olds having sex, need counseling, not birth control.

12

Random Drug Testing Violates Students' Rights

Debra J. Saunders

Debra J. Saunders is a conservative columnist whose work has appeared in the San Francisco Chronicle, Wall Street Journal, National Review, *in other mainstream publications, and on Web sites.*

Government should be kept out of family decision-making and parental responsibility, including the issue of student drug use. Because drug tests for all students would violate many edicts set forth in the U.S. Constitution (such as the presumption of innocence and the need for probable cause before conducting searches), court and school officials used a pretense of safety to begin testing student athletes for drugs. And then the officials— including the U.S. Supreme Court—stretched the justification for drug testing to cover any student who engages in extracurricular activities. Random student drug testing is wrong; it does not work, and it should be stopped.

In America, where citizens are supposed to want to keep government out of their family decision-making, there should be no random drug testing at public schools. Yet some 19 percent of public schools engage in some form of student drug testing, the University of Michigan's *Journal of School Health* found in 2003. President [George W.] Bush proposes to spend $25 million in 2006 to fund more random drug testing. And the internationally minded U.S. Supreme Court thinks that drug testing in public schools is just swell.

This is wrong. Parents who suspect their children of using drugs are free to test their kids. Hence, there is no need for schools to intervene—any more than there is a need for schools to set the punishment for children who disobey their parents' rules. Except that it is happening.

It would be a coercive violation of privacy rights to force all public-school students to submit to drug tests.

How It Started

It started when schools began testing athletes; there was at least the pretense of a safety argument for the tests—you don't want stoned kids leaping for a high fly [a tricky catch in baseball]. But by the time the U.S. Supreme Court ruled on said tests in 1995, the rationale for the tests had expanded. The [justices on the high court's] Big Bench supported testing of athletes to prevent the "increased risk of sports-related injury," but also because athletes are role models.

Court and school officials understand that it would be a coercive violation of privacy rights to force all public-school students to submit to drug tests. It goes against the presumption of innocence, unreasonable searches, the need for probable cause and other quaint notions found in the U. S. constitution. So those officials who want the government to play parent have come up with a new angle—require students who engage in extracurricular activities to agree to random drug testing. It's not mandatory, they argue, because students don't have to join clubs. And believe it or not, [in 2002 the U.S. Supreme court agreed].

The surest bet in America is: Once a bad idea is born, it only gets bigger.

Testifying before a House committee in February [2005], Bush drug czar John Walters argued that school "drug testing can be done effectively and compassionately." Its purpose, he explained, "is not to punish students who use drugs, but to prevent use in the first place, and to make sure users get the help they need to stop placing themselves and their friends at risk."

It Does Not Make Sense

[The problem] is: It is not clear how many students don't use drugs because they want to be in the chess club. Probably some students refrain. Still, University of Michigan researcher Lloyd Johnston noted in 2003 that there is "a serious question of whether drug testing is a wise investment," as it is not clear that it deters student drug use.

I don't think it is good policy to treat innocent students as if they might be guilty by making them pee in a cup if they want to be in debate club.

Meanwhile, there can be little doubt that students who use drugs say no to extracurricular activities because they don't want to say no to drugs. Testing for club membership, said Tom Angell of Students for Sensible Drug Policy, pushes these students "away from those positive atmospheres that study after study has shown are successful at keeping students away from drugs."

It's twisted: The very do-gooders who first lament that drug use consigns students to do poorly in school, now push for policies that marginalize students and guarantee that they will not have a full high-school experience.

And it doesn't matter what parents think. When the Supreme Court ruled in favor of testing for students who sign up for extracurricular activities in 2002, I asked the National School Board Association what it thought of a policy that required testing of students, even if parents took the responsibility. "The answer is that your child cannot participate in extracurricular activities," an official answered. "It's not negotiable."

Lori Earls, the parent of an Oklahoma high-school student on the losing side of the 2002 case, was outraged by the school's drug policy. She believed that other parents supported drug testing because it relieved them of the responsibility of their children's drug use, and ceded it to the schools. "They took away the parents' job," she noted.

And yet there is no outcry.

13

Students Should Be Tested for Drugs

David G. Evans

David G. Evans, executive director of the Drug Free Schools Coalition, is a member of the Student Drug-Testing Coalition. He also authored a successful amici curiae brief submitted to the Supreme Court in the case that expanded random student drug testing coverage to all students involved in extracurricular activities.

It is important that schools provide a safe environment for children so they can learn and grow academically, emotionally, and socially. The presence of drugs destroys that environment. And so, after an alarming number of students began using and selling drugs on school campuses, the U.S. Supreme Court ruled in favor of random drug testing for students involved in athletics and extracurricular activities. The goal is to deter drug use and protect the health and safety of students, a goal that far outweighs any cry of privacy violation.

Recently [2002], the United States Supreme Court came out with a commonsense ruling in favor of student drug testing. The Court decided that the health and safety of schools and students outweighed an individual student's minimal privacy interest when it comes to drug testing. The Court upheld a school drug testing program that permitted random testing of students in athletics and extracurricular activities such as clubs. The Court spoke of the drug use "epidemic" that is de-

David G. Evans, "Student Drug Testing Works," Student Drug-Testing Coalition, December 30, 2006. Reproduced by permission.

stroying the lives of thousands of children a year and wreaking havoc with their families. In the face of this destruction, the Court said that it is reasonable to use drug testing to deter drug use as we do in the military, workplace, criminal justice system, and professional athletics.

Drugs Are Insidious

When drugs invade a school, threatening the safety of students and disturbing the orderly learning environment, the school's interest in ridding the school of drugs outweighs the privacy interests of students. The school years are a critical passage in a young person's life. While in school, children face the challenge of learning in the academic, social, physical, and emotional realms. When drugs infect a school it cripples the learning process. Children become casualties. The physical and psychological effects of drug and alcohol use can cause lifelong and profound losses. Substance use decreases a child's chances of graduation and academic success.

Researchers continually report statistics demonstrating that student drug and alcohol use is at a dangerous level. For example, the National Center on Addiction and Substance Abuse (CASA) at Columbia University in New York City reports that for the last six years schoolchildren in the USA have listed drugs as the most important problem they face.

A 1997 CASA survey revealed that high school students see more drug deals at school than in their neighborhoods. In the survey, 76% of high school students claim that drugs are kept, used, or sold on school grounds. In addition, 29% of high school students claim that a student in their school died from a drug- or alcohol-related incident in the past year.

CASA also reports that substance abuse adds at least $41 billion dollars to the costs of elementary and secondary education in terms of special education, teacher turnover, truancy, property damage, injury, counseling, and other costs.

According to a study in the *Journal of the American Medical Association*, students who use drugs are more likely to bring guns and knives to school, leading to school violence. According to the New Jersey Department of Education report, assaults are up 30% with school staff as victims in 19% of the cases.

Students report that drug testing gives them a reason to say "no" to drugs.

Random Drug Testing Benefits All Students

Random drug testing is intended to give schools a stronger weapon to get drugs out of schools. School drug-testing programs are a proven low cost method to win the fight for our children's future. Consider the results of random drug testing of athletes at Hunterdon Central Regional High School in Flemington, New Jersey, USA. After two years of testing they experienced a decline in 20 of 28 categories of drug use in the whole student population. Studies in Oregon and Indiana in the USA also show substantial reductions in drug use due to testing.

The critics of testing claim that giving drug tests to students who participate in extracurricular activities will make the activities less attractive to students. They claim that by having less participation in extracurricular activities that students will choose to participate in drug-related behavior. While it is true that extracurricular activities help students to lead a positive life, there is no evidence that there is a drop-off in participation because of drug testing. In fact, students report that drug testing gives them a reason to say "no" to drugs. We must remember that the majority of kids do not use drugs!

The Court based its reasoning, in part, on the fact that these extracurricular activities are voluntary. If students wish to avoid a drug test, they can do so easily by not participating in these activities. We want students to make choices such as "do I use a drug or do I stay on the football team?" Our experience is that students choose the extracurricular activity over the drug. During the first year of random testing, the Hunterdon Central [High School] football team won the state championship. The coaches reported that the students were doing better in practice, and the students reported that drug testing gave them the opportunity to avoid drug parties.

Some critics say that extracurricular activities are a requirement to get into college and [that] students should not be forced to choose between extracurricular activities and their beliefs about their privacy. School-based extracurricular activities are not needed to get into college. There are many activities outside of school, such as athletics, plays, competitions like chess clubs, or service work.

Student testing should also include alcohol, although there is less need for alcohol testing because it is usually apparent when someone is under the influence of alcohol, which is not always the case with drug use.

Privacy Is Protected

The goals of random drug testing are to deter drug use and, if a student is detected as using drugs, to offer education and treatment to the student. The goal is not to punish students. This was specifically noted by the Supreme Court in approving such programs.

Student confidentiality is protected by two important federal laws. The first is the Family Educational Rights and Privacy Act. [It] prohibits student records from being released, including drug and alcohol testing results, without the consent of the parents or, if the student is 18, without the student's consent. Student treatment records are protected by the federal Alcohol and Drug Patient Regulations that carry federal criminal penalties for improperly releasing information.

Drug testing is not the final solution. Certainly we need to continue efforts at education and resolving our cultural problem with drugs. Drug testing only works when included in treatment and education.

For every student who claims that privacy is violated by having to take a drug test, we can show . . . parents who have buried their children because of drugs. [Schools] must be allowed to fulfill their mission of educating students and protecting [students'] health and safety. Drug testing is a valuable tool in achieving these goals.

14

Children Have the Right to Be Protected from Bullying

Ceil Than

Ceil Than is a writer, editor, and educator who has published fiction and nonfiction on a variety of topics.

A child who deliberately and consistently uses physical assault or verbal abuse to inflict fear or harm is a bully. Usually this behavior can begin as early as age eight, can be found in boys or girls, can take place anywhere children gather (including the Internet), and can cause extreme suffering and long-lasting emotional devastation for its victims. Because every child has the right to feel safe, parents, teachers, and school officials must learn to recognize the warning signs of bullying and create effective policies for dealing with and preventing such behavior.

Ask a twelve-year-old what he or she hates most about school, and you might be surprised to learn that the school bully outranks homework and tests on the fear-factor scale. A bully is a child who deliberately and [continually] uses physical assault or verbal abuse to harm another child that he or she sees as more vulnerable. Bullies and their victims can be as young as eight years old, and school bullying peaks in the high school years. Bullies and their victims can be boys or girls, and bullying can take place in cyberspace as well as [on] the schoolyard. Both the bully and his or her victim suffer, and some are driven to extreme or suicidal behavior.

Ceil Than, "'Wanna Fight?' Bullies and Their Victims Disarmed," Children's Rights of New York, Inc. *HOTLINE*, vol. 29, Spring 2008, pp. 1–3. Reproduced by permission.

According to a survey done by the American Academy of Child and Adolescent Psychiatry, 50% of school age children report being bullied at some point during their school years, and 10% report being bullied [continually]. Children in this age group are most intensely aware of their peers' opinions, acceptance, and rejection. The experience of being singled out and picked on can turn into an even more emotionally devastating downward spiral, and the experience of power felt by a bully can also become a dangerous emotional high that pushes him or her to more extreme behavior.

Children who are bullied have a higher absentee rate because the bullying makes them feel physically sick.

Bullying takes place anywhere children gather: the playground, the cafeteria, the school hallways, the school bus, the mall, online on websites such as MySpace, or on cell phones via calls and text messaging. Bullying takes the form of punching, hitting, tripping, name-calling, posting embarrassing messages or photographs, or sending nasty messages. Bullies can be boys or girls, known or unknown to their victims.

Who Are the Victims?

Children who are bullied are often singled out because they are seen as different; that is, nerdy, overweight, or too shy, of a different race or background, the new kid in school, or physically or mentally challenged. According to an essay by Karen Gouze, Ph.D., on the Children's Memorial Hospital website, even more damaging than physical assault is "indirect" or "relational" bullying that involves isolating the victim from the group by spreading false rumors about him or her, or ignoring him or her. This type of bullying has been intensified by the use of the Internet and it is more difficult for parents and teachers to spot. The WebMD site (www.webmd.com) reports that children who are bullied have a higher absentee rate because the bullying makes them feel physically sick, and they wanted to avoid going to school and encountering the bully.

April Himes of Poteau, Oklahoma, was a typical middle-school student. However, she had been singled out by her peers and teased because of her appearance. The teasing continued so long and so intensely that she committed suicide rather than go to school and face her tormentors one more day. On the memorial website posted by her parents, there is a gallery of seven other children from across the United States who were also bullied into the extreme response of suicide.

Bullying escalates the longer it goes unreported.

What Are the Warning Signs?

Parents are cautioned to watch for indications that their child has been bullied, such as:

- depression, feelings of worthlessness

- anxiety, nausea, fear of going to school

- sleeplessness, nightmares

- withdrawal from family, friends and activities that were always pleasurable.

However, Dr. Gouze also encourages pediatricians in particular to help parents "build children's resilience." From the time their children are preschoolers, parents should

- foster self-esteem in their children,

- teach them to respect others and interact . . . in socially acceptable ways,

- model how to respond assertively, but not aggressively, to negative comments,

- encourage them to buddy up with other children as a support system, and

- teach them to know when to tell an adult about negative behaviors that they experience or observe.

The final step is crucial because bullying escalates the longer it goes unreported, and no one steps in to stop the behavior. Delayed intervention hurts the bully as much as the child being bullied.

Who Are the Bullies?

Children may become bullies because they have been the victims of bullying. According to 2001 study by psychologist Tonja Nansel, Ph.D., 6% of the 15,000 U.S. sixth- through tenth-graders she surveyed responded that they had been both bullies and the victims of bullies. Bullies may be emotionally immature and insecure, and [they may] lack social skills and the ability to take responsibility for their actions or choices. According to www.kidshealth.org, if a bully continues his or her aggressive behavior past his or her late teens, he or she not only risks losing friends who now view such behavior as immature, but also risks becoming the one out of every four elementary school bullies [who] has a criminal record by the time he or she is thirty years old.

Episodes of school shootings have been linked to bullying, as former victims of bullying were so emotionally distressed that they resorted to an extreme and violent form of bullying as a response to the treatment they received. The Secret Service and the U.S. Department of Education investigated 37 school shootings across the country and discovered that 66% of student gunmen stated that they had been bullied.

Dylan Klebold and Eric Harris, the teenage gunmen who killed 12 students and a teacher and injured 23 others before killing themselves in the 1999 Columbine High School shootings, left writings detailing the bullying they felt led to their behavior. However, according to Jordan Peterson, a professor at the University of Toronto and a clinical psychologist, this type of extreme response is not the norm, but a result of someone who is "profoundly alienated." In his interview with CTV.ca News, Peterson stated that everyone experiences "hurt, loss, or rejection" in their lives, but most find non-violent ways to overcome those experiences.

What Are the Warning Signs?

Just as parents should watch for signs that their child has been the victim of a bully, parents should watch for signs that their child might be becoming a bully such as:

- Withdrawal from family, friends, and activities that were always pleasurable

- Feelings of worthlessness, friendlessness

- Physical or verbal aggression, i.e. pushing, hitting, or name-calling

- Lack of sympathy for a child who has been hurt or teased

- Lying

- Lack of contact with other children, such as fewer invitations to join classmates' parties or games, and

- Sudden possession of new toys, gadgets, or money that he or she bullied classmates into handing over

Some of the warning signs for bullies and their victims are similar, such as withdrawal from family and friends. The same methods of building "resilience" in a potential victim of bullying will work to help a child avoid becoming a bully. Helping a child find positive and acceptable ways to deal with anxiety, frustration, and anger can keep him or her from the emotional and social alienation that can deepen until the child lashes out in an extreme response.

Schools across the United States lack uniform and effective policies for dealing with and preventing bullying. Although parents should contact their child's teacher and school administration for help in dealing with bullying, parents are the best means of defense, and early intervention is crucial. Parents must learn to recognize the warning signs of their children being bullied or becoming bullies, take these signs seriously, and act to help their children find ways to deal with the problem. No child should be afraid to go to school or be so angry with his or her classmates that he or she targets them for harm or harassment.

15

Punishment Therapy Violates the Rights of Children with Disabilities

The Alliance to Prevent Restraint, Aversive Interventions, and Seclusion (APRAIS)

The Alliance to Prevent Restraint, Aversive Interventions, and Seclusion (APRAIS) was established in 2004 by leading education, research, and advocacy organizations to protect children with significant disabilities from abuse in schools, treatment programs, and residential facilities.

Every day, children with disabilities or challenging behaviors are routinely subjected to painful and traumatizing treatment by licensed caregivers. To make matters worse, these abusive treatments—such as hitting or punching a child, restraining a child so that he or she cannot move, or locking a child in a closet—have been shown to cause more harm than good, spawning children who feel helpless, frustrated, angry, or violent while the underlying cause goes undetected and unresolved. The use of such abusive techniques on children should be considered cruel and unusual punishment, thereby a violation of the Eighth Amendment to the United States Constitution.

Every day in this country, children with disabilities are needlessly being subjected to harmful practices in the name of treating "challenging behaviors." They are brought down to the ground and straddled, strapped or tied in chairs and beds, blindfolded slapped and pinched, startled by cold water sprays in the face, deprived of food, secluded in locked rooms, and more, despite the fact that research and practice show that these techniques exacerbate challenging behavior and do nothing to teach the child appropriate behaviors. . . .

The deliberate use of pain, humiliation, exclusion, and immobilization on a child has all the hallmarks of abuse.

Across the country, teachers, aides, and program staff who have been entrusted with children's care, protection, education, and development are subjecting them to this "treatment." In fact, such negative and dangerous activities are often inappropriately included as part of these children's education plans in the hope that they will reduce the occurrence of unwanted behavior. Children learn nothing about acceptable behavior from the experience of being hurt, secluded, or immobilized by their caregivers. Children with serious communication, social, and behavior challenges need effective, research-based, positive approaches based on Positive Behavior Supports (PBS). PBS teaches desired behaviors [and] useful skills, and fosters healthy emotional development and interactions with others. PBS is widely accepted as effective evidence-based practice that not only reduces even the most dangerous and disruptive behaviors, but focuses on the vision of quality of life.

Sanctioned Abuse

Many parents are unaware that their children are being routinely hurt, restrained, secluded, and subjected to painful and ineffective practices by their school or program. Some have signed vague or confusing consent forms which offered no clear picture of the dangerous interventions planned for their child. Other parents are aware of and deeply troubled by the methods used on their child, but have been threatened with loss of the placement or other essential services if they object.

The deliberate use of pain, humiliation, exclusion, and immobilization on a child has all the hallmarks of abuse. Most parents assume that a child with disabilities has the same protections against abuse that other children are given. Unfortunately, the programmatic application of these abusive procedures on children with disabilities is often treated differently. In many special education programs and service delivery systems the use of pain and humiliation (aversive interventions) and immobilization (restraint and seclusion) to control or change behavior is state-sanctioned—allowed under a confusing patchwork of outdated, poorly written, or overly permissive laws and regulations. When abuse is permitted in this way, parents may find that the usual responses to child endangerment, such as seeking help from school administrators, the police, or the courts, fail to solve the immediate threat their child is facing. When abuse is sanctioned, it becomes less visible. Injuries and deaths involving these procedures are believed to be significantly underreported. The kinds of investigations that would expose the nature and extent of the problem are seldom done, and accurate information based on medical or forensic reporting is difficult to obtain. The deaths and injuries of children with disabilities are too easily blamed on accidents or on aspects of the disability itself. But in recent years parents are speaking out, and advocacy organizations, legislators, and the courts are realizing the seriousness of this threat to the basic human rights of vulnerable children and youth.

Aversive interventions, restraint, and seclusion are used on children across the spectrum of disabilities, including those with autism, learning disabilities, mental health needs, cognitive challenges, and children with physical and sensory disabilities. Schools and programs continue to use aversive interventions, restraint, and seclusion for a variety of unacceptable reasons, for example: because they are understaffed; for staff convenience; because they think "bad behavior" should be punished; because they do not believe the children they serve have the same needs, rights, and feelings as children who do not have disability labels; or because the school or program lacks leadership and does not empower teachers and staff with the knowledge, support, and positive alternatives they need.

The use of aversives, restraint and seclusion has resulted in hundreds of deaths and thousands of injuries. Even when no physical harm is apparent, these techniques cause psychological trauma and rob people of their dignity.

Types of Abusive Treatment

Aversive interventions (or "aversives") involve the deliberate infliction of physical and/or emotional pain and suffering, for the purpose of changing or controlling a child's behavior. Aversives include (but are not limited to) techniques such as direct physical or corporal punishment (hitting or pinching); visual screening; forcing a child to inhale or ingest noxious substances; sensory deprivation; depriving a child of food, use of a toilet, or other health-sustaining necessities; and temporarily but significantly depriving a child of the ability to move. Use of restraint devices as well as blindfolds, visual screens, and white noise helmets results in sensory deprivation. Techniques that deliberately disrupt a child's basic emotional well-being and sense of safety, or that result in the long-term loss of the normal freedoms and pleasures of childhood by preventing exercise, peer interactions or other activities may also be considered aversive.

Restraint is a type of aversive that involves the forced restriction or immobilization of the child's body or parts of the body, contingent on a designated behavior. There are three types of restraint. Manual restraint involves various "holds" for grabbing and immobilizing a child or bringing a child to the floor. The child is kept in the chosen restraint position by one or more staff person's arms, legs, or body weight. Mechanical restraint is the use of straps, cuffs, mat and blanket wraps, helmets, and other devices to prevent movement and/or sense perception, often by pinning the child's limbs to a splint, wall, bed, chair, or floor. Chemical restraint means using medication to stop behavior by dulling a child's ability to move and/or think. Medication specifically prescribed to treat symptoms of a disability or illness is not a chemical restraint.

It is generally accepted that brief physical intervention used to interrupt an immediate and serious danger to the child or others may be called for in the case of safety emergency. This is different from the ongoing use of restraint as punishment or in the guise of treatment for a child's disability or behavior. Frequent use of emergency restraint is an indication [that] program revision is needed, even if the program is considered positive.

Seclusion involves forced isolation in a room or space from which the child cannot escape. Allowing a child to voluntarily take a break from activities is not considered seclusion.

A child who is squirted in the face each time he or she screams is not learning new and better ways to communicate.

Long-Term Behavioral Problems

Positive behavior interventions are safe in the short run, and in the long run promote habits and attitudes that continue to reduce risk. On the other hand, aversive interventions, restraint, and seclusion may cause injury and death, and they can backfire in ways that cannot be predicted or controlled. According to the professional literature, the following are some crucial considerations in choosing safe, respectful, and effective interventions:

• Children generalize what they learn. Anxiety and avoidance triggered by aversives, restraint, and seclusion will spread to other areas of a child's life and become an obstacle to achieving desirable behaviors, attitudes, and progress. For example, a child who experiences aversive procedures in the classroom will come to fear and avoid the classroom itself, the teacher, the school bus, the school, and the learning process in general.

• Children learn from their experiences with adults. Physically coercive activities teach children that "might makes right" and that physical means of problem-solving are acceptable. The small child who is easily restrained today will soon become a large, strong teenager able to demonstrate the dangerous behavior he/she has been taught.

• We can help a child best by seeking the underlying cause of his or her behavior. When aversive techniques, restraint, and seclusion are used to stop behavior for the short term, the real cause of that behavior goes undetected and unresolved. The underlying cause, whether medical, emotional, or social, is masked by these methods and can worsen as a result of the very techniques used.

• Adults can teach children alternate ways to communicate. Helping children learn new skills provides them with opportunities for achieving success. Aversive strategies, restraint, and seclusion do not offer [a] child useful alternative behaviors. For instance, a child who is squirted in the face each time he or she screams is not learning new and better ways to communicate with teachers and staff or to solve the problem that is causing the screams.

• Positive strategies can flourish only when negative interventions are rejected. The use of restraint, seclusion, and restrictive techniques take time, training, and imaginative energy away from the search for positive strategies for children with disabilities. Teachers or staff may be caught in a cycle of negative responses from which it becomes increasingly difficult to escape.

• Trusting relationships between a child and his or her teacher, combined with a sense of safety, are fundamental for healthy child development. Aversives, restraint, and seclusion eliminate the opportunity for such an environment or relationship.

• Children need to know that their bodies are their own, and that sometimes it is right to refuse or say "no." When children are taught that it is appropriate for adults to grab and hold them, and that a "good" child should submit without objection, these children can become easy victims for sexual predators.

• All children should enjoy equal protection from danger and risk. Children with disabilities are already three times more likely to be abused than children without disabilities. Permitting dangerous activities labeled as treatment leaves this vulnerable group with unequal protection under the law.

• When children with disabilities are taught alongside their typical peers, positive strategies are more likely to be the norm. Schools and programs that use aversives, restraint, and seclusion tend to operate in segregated settings, away from public view, because these dangerous interventions violate community standards and values.

Trauma and Child Development

Practitioners of aversive techniques, restraint, and seclusion used to believe that if the child was not physically injured by such interventions, they had done a safe job. Now we know better.

Advances in our understanding of child development emphasize the importance of a secure, well-balanced emotional life. A child repeatedly subjected to these techniques grows up feeling helpless, frightened, frustrated, or angry. The child's reactions may become increasingly stressed.

Over time, the overworked stress response system of the child's brain can become unbalanced, creating an ongoing state of high arousal. Repetitive, impulsive activity patterns, such as the "fight or flight" response, become locked in as the child's brain chemistry changes. The child becomes less able to control emotions, to pay attention, or to take in new information and use it to make appropriate decisions. Eventually, such a child may misinterpret even the well-intended actions of others as threatening.

These classic responses to trauma interrupt and can permanently alter brain development. They fuel a downward spiral in which teachers or program staff are both creating and responding to the child's anger and inflexibility.

No Justifiable Reasons

There are no justifiable reasons for using aversive interventions, restraint, and seclusion. Law and regulations covering most children's service delivery systems generally agree that aversive interventions, restraint, and seclusion may not be used for purposes of staff convenience, or as coercion, punishment, or retaliation. These methods are not "teaching" methods because they do not teach positive behaviors. The use of aversive interventions, restraint, and seclusion under the guise of therapeutic or educational interventions is unethical because these procedures create risk and unnecessarily take away basic rights. There is a lack of evidence that aversive techniques offer a safe means of teaching desirable, self-directed behavior that a child can maintain over the long term. Safe, positive methods of changing and redirecting behavior are well-documented. Evidence shows them to be successful regardless of the child's diagnostic label, degree of disability, or severity of behaviors. The responsibility to employ best practices and the obligation to do no harm in treatment require that the least dangerous, least intrusive, and least restrictive methods always be used.

Individual liberty is protected under the doctrine of least restrictive alternative (LRA). LRA requires careful consideration of the individual's interests; the purpose of treatment; and the interventions and environments chosen to provide treatment. Additionally, interventions must be demonstrated as effective for the purpose for which they are used, and there must be proof of therapeutic justification. LRA, therefore, provides parents and advocates a strong constitutionally based argument in favor of positive interventions over the use of aversive interventions, restraint, and seclusion—all highly restrictive procedures. . . .

The use of aversives, non-emergency restraint, and seclusion in facilities run by federal, state, or local governments raises important issues of constitutional protections. Some courts have ruled against the use of these behavioral interventions on people with disabilities on the grounds that [doing so violates] the Eighth Amendment prohibition against "cruel and unusual punishment." Other legal decisions have found the Eighth Amendment to apply only to prisons and other penal facilities. This leads to a seemingly indefensible predicament: certain aversives and restraints permitted for "therapeutic" use on children with disabilities are considered too inhumane to be constitutionally applied as punishments in prisons.

Unjustified restraint use in public facilities has been successfully challenged as a violation of constitutionally protected liberty interests under the Fourteenth Amendment. The Supreme Court (in *Youngberg v. Romeo*, 1982) found that a man with mental retardation who was committed to a state facility had constitutional rights, including a right to reasonably safe conditions of confinement, freedom from unreasonable bodily restraints, and minimally adequate training. The Supreme

Court thus adopted the position that persons involuntarily committed "retain liberty interests in freedom of movement and in personal security" and that providers risk liability when they use aversives or restraints.

16

Children's Rights Should Be Considered with Regard to Parenthood

Elizabeth Marquardt

Elizabeth Marquardt is the director of the Center for Marriage and Families at the Institute for American Values in New York and the author of Between Two Worlds: The Inner Lives of Children of Divorce.

A clash between adult rights and children's needs with regard to parenthood and conception is emerging throughout the world. With the advent of assisted reproductive technologies—for example, in vitro fertilization, DNA experimentation, and stem cell research for cloning—along with the already established practices of adoption and legal guardianship, governments and societies are altering the traditional definition of parenthood by using such terms as "natural parent," "legal parent," "psychological parent," or even "Progenitor A and Progenitor B." While all of this is going on, the fundamental rights and best interest of the children are becoming lost. More time and research should be devoted to understanding the needs of children before new laws change the time-honored definition of parenthood.

Around the world, the two-person, mother-father model of parenthood is being fundamentally challenged.

In Canada, with virtually no debate, the controversial law that brought about same-sex marriage quietly included the provision to erase the term "natural parent" across the board in federal law, replacing it with the term "legal parent." With that law, the locus of power in defining who a child's parents are shifts precipitously from civil society to the state, with the consequences as yet unknown.

In Spain, after the recent legalization of same-sex marriage, the legislature changed the birth certificates for all children in that nation to read "Progenitor A" and "Progenitor B" instead of "mother" and "father." With that change, the words "mother" and "father" were struck from the first document issued to every newborn by the state. Similar proposals have been made in other jurisdictions that have legalized same-sex marriage.

In New Zealand and Australia, influential law commissions have proposed allowing children conceived with use of sperm or egg donors to have three legal parents. Yet neither group addresses the real possibility that a child's three legal parents could break up and feud over the child's best interests.

Courts often must determine who the legal parents are among the many adults who might be involved in planning, conceiving, birthing, and raising a child.

In the United States, courts often must determine who the legal parents are among the many adults who might be involved in planning, conceiving, birthing, and raising a child. In a growing practice, judges in several states have seized upon the idea of "psychological" parenthood to award legal parent status to adults who are not related to children by blood, adoption, or marriage. At times they have done so even over the objection of the child's biological parent. Also, successes in the same-sex marriage debate have encouraged group marriage advocates who wish to break open the two-person understanding of marriage and parenthood.

Scientists Get Involved

Meanwhile, scientists around the world are experimenting with the DNA in eggs and sperm in nearly unimaginable ways, raising the specter of children born with one or three genetic parents, or two same-sex parents. Headlines recently announced research at leading universities in Britain and New Zealand that could enable same-sex couples or single people to procreate. In Britain, scientists were granted permission to create embryos with three genetic parents. Stem cell research has introduced the very real possibility that a cloned child could be born—and the man who pioneered in vitro fertilization (IVF) treatment has already said in public that cloning should be offered to childless couples who have exhausted other options. The list goes on.

Nearly all of these steps, and many more, are being taken in the name of adult rights to form families they choose. But what about the children? . . .

At stake are the most elemental features of children's well-being—their social and physical health and their moral and spiritual wholeness.

Questions Arise Concerning Adult Rights Versus Child Need

Right now, our societies urgently require reflection, debate, and research about the policies and practices that will serve the best interests of children—those already born and those yet to be born. This report argues that around the world the state is taking an increasingly active role in defining and regulating parenthood far beyond its limited, vital, historic, and child-centered role in finding suitable parents for needy children through adoption. The report documents how the state creates new uncertainties and vulnerabilities when it increasingly seeks to administer parenthood, often giving far greater attention to adult rights than to children's needs. For the most part, this report does not advocate for or against particular policy prescriptions (such as banning donor conception) but rather seeks to draw urgently needed public attention to the current revolutionary changes in parenthood, to point out the risks and contradictions arising from increased state intervention, and to insist that our societies immediately undertake a vigorous, child-centered debate.

Children have a right and need to know their origins.

Do mothers and fathers matter to children? Is there anything special—anything worth supporting—about the two-person, mother-father model? Are children commodities to be produced by the marketplace? What role should the state have in defining parenthood? When adult rights clash with children's needs, how should the conflict be resolved? These are the questions raised by this report. Our societies will either answer these questions democratically and as a result of intellectually and morally serious reflection and public debate, or we will find, very soon, that these questions have already been answered for us. The choice is ours. At stake are the most elemental features of children's well-being—their social and physical health and their moral and spiritual wholeness. . . .

Government Plays an Active Role in Defining Parenthood

At this moment, with virtually no public discussion, the relationship that is most core and vital to children's very survival—that of parenthood—is being fundamentally redrawn through new laws, proposals, and practices affecting marriage, reproduction, and family life, with the state playing an increasingly active role in defining parenthood for broader categories of children.

Given that in some ways the genie is already out of the bottle, it is not entirely clear what actions the state and social leaders should take in the near future. For instance, some nations have moved to ban the practice of anonymous donation of sperm and eggs. This would seem to be a positive development for children—after all, there is a strong argument to be made that children have a right and need to know their origins. Yet greater acceptance of the idea that donor-conceived children have a right to know their origins is also leading to the idea that these children should have the possibility of some kind of *relationship* with their sperm or egg donor (and not just a file of information), or even that the donor should have some kind of legal parental status in the child's life, ... as in New Zealand and Australia, where commissions have proposed allowing donors to "opt in" as children's third legal parents.

What might the future hold for children with three or more legal parents? We have no idea.

Or, in another example, after Britain passed a law banning donor anonymity there was a purported drastic drop in the number of men willing to donate sperm. The state health service then began an active campaign to recruit sperm and egg donors, no longer just allowing the intentional conception of children who will not know or be raised in relationship with their own biological parents, but very intentionally promoting it. Meanwhile, couples in that nation who wish to conceive have even greater incentive to go abroad to nations or regions that have less regulation—such as Spain, India, Eastern Europe, or elsewhere—to procure sperm or eggs or surrogate wombs, making it even less likely that their child will ever be able to trace their origins or form a relationship with a distant donor abroad.

Again, how will these developments affect children? At the moment we have no real idea. But we certainty do have serious and immediate cause for concern.

Research About Children's Well-Being
Is Necessary

For reasons like these, this report does not conclude with the usual list of specific policy recommendations. Rather, this report issues a call to fellow citizens in the United States and Canada and around the world. The call is for all of us to participate in urgently needed conversation and research about the revolution in parenthood and the needs of children.

When there is a clash between adult rights and children's needs, the children should take precedence.

This much is clear: When society changes marriage, it changes parenthood. The divorce revolution and the rise in single-parent childbearing weakened ties of fathers to their children and introduced a host of players at times called "parents." The use of assisted reproductive technologies by married heterosexual couples—and later by singles and same-sex couples—raised still more uncertainties about the meaning of motherhood and fatherhood and exposed children to new losses the adults never fathomed. The legalization of same-sex marriage, while sometimes seen as a small change affecting just a few people, raises the startling prospect of fundamentally breaking the legal institution of marriage from any ties to biological parenthood. Meanwhile, successes in the same-sex marriage debate have encouraged others who wish fully and completely to break open the two-person understanding of marriage and parenthood.

Here is where we are. In law and culture, the two-natural-parent, mother-father model is falling away, replaced with the idea that children are fine with any one or more adults being called their parents, so long as the appointed parents are nice people. This change is happening incrementally, largely led by self-appointed experts and advocates in a few fields. But it does not have to be this way. Those of us who are concerned can and should take up and lead a debate about the lives of children and the future of parenthood.

As we launch this conversation, a guiding principle could be this: When there is a clash between adult rights and children's needs, the interests of the more vulnerable party—in this case, the children—should take precedence. A great deal of evidence supports the idea that children, on average, do best when raised by their own, married mother and father, with adoption as an important, pro-child, admirable alternative. With regard to some newly visible family forms, such as families headed by gay or lesbian parents or those created using donor sperm, eggs, or surrogacy, we have more to learn more about the lasting, inner experience of the children.

To provide time and space for this conversation and for more research, this report also calls for a moratorium or a "time out" lasting five years. Until we better understand and prioritize the needs of children, no legislatures, courts, or commissions should press forward with recommendations or changes that broadly undermine the normative importance of mothers and fathers in the lives of children, nor should they support intentionally denying unborn children knowledge of and a relationship with their own mother and father. Rather, they should concentrate their energies on rigorous inquiry and active debate about the needs of children and the role of mothers and fathers in their lives.

The well-being of the world's children calls us to act—not years from now but right now. For their sake, for those born and those yet to be born, we must be willing to launch a sometimes uncomfortable but urgent debate about the well-being of children born in an age that is rapidly redefining the meaning of parenthood. Nothing is inevitable. The time to act is now.

Organizations to Contact

The editors have compiled the following list of organizations concerned with the issues debated in this book. The descriptions are derived from materials provided by the organizations. All have publications or information available for interested readers. The list was compiled on the date of publication of the present volume; the information provided here may change. Be aware that many organizations take several weeks or longer to respond to inquiries, so allow as much time as possible.

Advocates for Youth
2000 M Street NW, Suite 750, Washington, DC   20036
(202) 419-3420 • fax: (202) 419-1448
e-mail: information@advocatesforyouth.org
Web site: www.advocatesforyouth.org

Advocates for Youth believes young people have the right to accurate and complete sexual health information to enable them to make healthy decisions about sexuality, and about confidential reproductive and sexual health services. The organization publishes fact sheets and brochures on adolescent behavior and sexuality including "Comprehensive Sex Education: Research and Results" and "Science and Success: Clinical Services and Contraceptive Access."

American Civil Liberties Union (ACLU)
125 Broad Street, 18th Floor, New York, NY   10004-2400
(212) 54-2500
e-mail: infoaclu@aclu.org
Web site: www.aclu.org

The ACLU is a national organization that works to defend Americans' civil rights guaranteed by the U.S. Constitution. Seeking to protect the rights of students and others, it opposes random school searches and drug testing, zero tolerance policies, racism, sexism, homophobia, and religious intolerance. The ACLU offers policy statements and pamphlets, and its *Blog of Rights* discusses many topics including reproductive freedom, and youth and schools.

Child Labor Coalition (CLC)

1701 K Street NW, Suite 1200, Washington, DC 20006
(202) 835-3323 • fax: (202) 835-0747
e-mail: childlabor@nclnet.org
Web site: stopchildlabor.org

The CLC, a group of more than twenty organizations, represents consumers, labor unions, educators, human rights and labor rights groups, child advocacy groups, and religious and women's groups. It was established in 1989 and is cochaired by the National Consumers League and the American Federation of Teachers. Its mission is to protect working youth and to promote legislation, programs, and initiatives to end child labor exploitation in the United States and abroad. The CLC's Web site offers news reports, press releases, and fact sheets, including "Children in the Fields: The Inequitable Treatment of Child Farmworkers" and "Youth Peddling Crews: Sweatshops of the Streets."

Children's Rights Information Network (CRIN)

East Studio, 2 Pontypool Place, London SE1 8QF
United Kingdom
+44-20-7401-2257
e-mail: info@crin.org
Web site: www.crin.org

CRIN is an international network of children's rights organizations that supports the effective exchange of information about children and their rights to help implement the United Nations Convention on the Rights of the Child. The network publishes information on children's rights, including "Children and Adolescents Statement: Strategies for International Cooperation" and "Haiti: Lost Childhoods in Haiti."

Child Trends

4301 Connecticut Ave. NW, Suite 350, Washington, DC 20008
(202) 572-6000 • fax: (202) 362-8420
Web site: www.childtrends.org

Child Trends is a nonprofit, nonpartisan research center that studies children at all stages of development. The organization works to improve outcomes for children by providing research, data, and analysis to the people and institutions whose decisions and actions affect children, including program providers, the policy community, researchers and educators, and the media. Founded in 1979, Child Trends helps keep the nation focused on children and their needs by identifying emerging issues; evaluating important programs and policies; and providing data-driven, evidence-based guidance on policy and practice. In addition to the newsletter *Facts at a Glance*, which presents the latest data on sexual behavior and teen pregnancy for cities and states, and the periodic newsletter *The Child Indicator*, CT also publishes fact sheets, including *Contraceptive Use Patterns Across Teens' Sexual Relationships* and *Neighborhood Support and Children's Connectedness*.

Committee on the Rights of the Child (CRC)

Office of the United Nations High Commissioner
  for Human Rights, Palais des Nations
Geneva 10 CH-1211
  Switzerland
+41 22-928-92-24 • fax: +41 22-928-90-10
Web site: www2.ohchr.org/english/bodies/crc

The CRC is a body of independent experts that monitors implementation of the United Nations Convention on the Rights of the Child by governments that have ratified the convention. The committee is made up of eighteen members from different countries who are considered to be experts in the field of human rights. The CRC publishes sessional and annual reports, press releases, and meeting summaries.

Education World
1062 Barnes Road, Suite 301, Wallingford, CT   06492
e-mail: webmaster@educationworld.com
Web site: www.educationworld.com

Education World is a site where teachers and administrators share ideas, find research materials, and read daily columns. Educators can browse hundreds of articles written by education experts covering such topics as dress codes, drug education, and school safety. The organization prints twelve newsletters, including *Weekly Newsletter: What's New This Week?* and *Headlines Newsletter.*

Freechild Project
PO Box 6185, Olympia, WA   98507-6185
(360) 489-9680
e-mail: info@freechild.org
Web site: www.freechild.org

The Freechild Project is a think tank, resource agency, and advocacy group for young people around the world who seek to play a larger role in their schools and communities. Training and conferences are offered to help parents, teachers, and community leaders involve youth in their communities. The Freechild Project publishes booklets, fact sheets, speeches, and book reviews, and its resources directory offers a wealth of information about school uniforms, zero tolerance, free speech, and student equality.

Human Rights Watch
350 Fifth Ave., New York, NY   10118-3299
(212) 290-4700 • fax: (212) 736-1300
e-mail: hrwnyc@hrw.org
Web site: www.hrw.org

Human Rights Watch is an activist organization dedicated to protecting the human rights of people around the world, including workers' rights. It investigates and exposes human rights violations and holds abusers accountable. It publishes an annual world report, and in its Children's Rights section has published "U.S.: Adopt Stronger Laws for Child Farmworkers" and "Indonesia: Protect Child Domestic Workers."

National Labor Committee (NLC)
5 Gateway Center, 6th Floor, Pittsburgh, PA   15222
(412) 562-2406 • fax: (412) 562-2411
e-mail: nlc@nlcnet.org
Web site: www.nlcnet.org

The committee seeks to educate and actively engage the U.S. public on human and labor rights abuses by corporations. Through education and activism, it works to end labor and human rights violations, ensure a living wage, and help workers and their families live and work with dignity. It produces videos, posters, and reports, including "Broken Lives: Behind U.S. Production in China," and "Child Labor Is Back."

Save the Children
54 Wilton Road, Westport, CT   06880
(800) 728-3843
Web site: www.savethechildren.org

Save the Children is an independent organization that seeks to ensure every child's right to survival, protection, education, and health. The organization publishes newsletters, research reports, issue briefs, fact sheets, and policy reports, including "Rewrite the Future: Education for Children in Conflict-Affected Countries."

Students for Sensible Drug Policy (SSDP)
1623 Connecticut Ave. NW, Suite 300, Washington, DC   20009
(202) 293-4414 • fax: (202) 293-8344
e-mail: ssdp@ssdp.org
Web site: www.ssdp.org

Students for Sensible Drug Policy is an international grassroots network of students who are concerned about the impact drug abuse has on communities, but who also know that the War on Drugs is failing. SSDP mobilizes and empowers young people to participate in the political process, pushing for sensible policies to achieve a safer and more just future, while fighting back against counterproductive Drug War policies, particularly ones that directly harm students and youth. SSDP prints pamphlets and flyers to encourage others to oppose drug testing in schools and to help change drug policies at the campus level.

United Nations Children's Fund (UNICEF)
UNICEF House, 3 United Nations Plaza, New York, NY   10017
(212) 686-5222 • fax: (212) 779-1679
e-mail: information@unicefusa.org
Web site: www.unicef.org

UNICEF, a nonpartisan organization, is mandated by the United Nations General Assembly to advocate for the protection of children's rights and to expand their opportunities. UNICEF upholds the Convention on the Rights of the Child and provides health care, clean water, improved nutrition, and education to millions of children worldwide. Among its publications are the yearly reports "The State of the World's Children," "Progress for Children," and the Annual Report, which spotlights significant results achieved on behalf of children around the world.

Bibliography

Books

Priscilla Alderson *Young Children's Rights: Exploring Beliefs, Principles and Practice, 2nd Edition.* Philadelphia, PA: Jessica Kingsley Publishers, 2008.

Barbara Coloroso *The Bully, the Bullied, and the Bystander: From Preschool to High School—How Parents and Teachers Can Help Break the Cycle.* New York: Harper Paperbacks, 2009.

Foundation Intervida *Exploited Lives: Child Labor Exploitation.* Barcelona, Spain: Intervida.org, 2008.

Michael D.A. Freeman *Children's Health and Children's Rights.* Boston: Nijoff Publishers, 2006.

James Garbarino and Ellen de Lara *And Words Can Hurt Forever: How to Protect Adolescents from Bullying, Harassment and Emotional Violence.* New York: Free Press, 2003.

Martin Guggenheim *What's Wrong with Children's Rights.* Cambridge, MA: Harvard University Press, 2005.

Wendy Herumin *Child Labor Today: A Human Rights Issue.* Berkeley Heights, NJ: Enslow Publishers, 2008.

Abigail Jones and
Marissa Miley

*Restless Virgins: Love, Sex, and
Survival at a New England Prep
School.* New York: HarperCollins,
2007.

Grace Ketterman

*Teaching Your Child About Sex: An
Essential Guide for Parents.* Grand
Rapids, MI: Revell, 2007.

Kathiann M.
Kowalski

*The Earls Case and the Student Drug
Testing Debate: Debating Supreme
Court Decisions.* Berkeley Heights, NJ:
Enslow Publishers, 2006.

Nicholas D.
Kristof and Sheryl
WuDunn

*Half the Sky: Turning Oppression into
Opportunity for Women Worldwide.*
New York: Alfred A. Knopf, 2009.

Bill O'Reilly and
Charles Flowers

Kids Are Americans Too. New York:
William Morrow, 2007.

John T. Pardeck

Children's Rights: Policy and Practice.
New York: Haworth Social Work
Practice Press, 2006.

Helena Silverstein

*Girls on the Stand: How Courts Fail
Pregnant Minors.* New York: New
York University Press, 2007.

Rosemarie Skaine

*Female Genital Mutilation: Legal,
Cultural and Medical Issues.* Jefferson,
NC: McFarland & Company, 2005.

Monica Feria
Tinta

*The Landmark Rulings of the
Inter-American Court of Human
Rights on the Rights of the Child:
Protecting the Most Vulnerable at the
Edge.* Boston: Nijoff Publishers, 2008.

| Jonathan Todres, Mark E. Wojcik, Cris R. Revaz | *The U.N. Convention on the Rights of the Child: An Analysis of Treaty Provisions and Implications of U.S. Ratification.* Ardsley, NY: Transnational Publishers, 2006. |

| Michael Wessells | *Child Soldiers: From Violence to Protection.* Cambridge, MA: Harvard University Press, 2007. |

| Barbara Bennett Woodhouse | *Hidden in Plain Sight: The Tragedy of Children's Rights from Ben Franklin to Lionel Tate.* Princeton, NJ: Princeton University Press, 2008. |

Periodicals

| Kat Aaron | "Minors Fight for the Right to Vote," *American Observer,* October 16, 2008. |

| Associated Press | "Rise in Bullying Has School Staffs in the Hot Seat: Most Not Trained to Handle It, Expert Says," March 31, 2010. |

| Zoe Chafe | "Child Labor Harms Many Young Lives," WorldWatch.org, November 8, 2007. |

| Mona Charen | "Yes, Abstinence Education: It's Still a Good Idea," *National Review,* September 3, 2008. |

| Victoria Clayton | "Parents, Experts Divided on School Drug Testing," MSNBC.com, September 21, 2007. |

E.R. Clough   "A Heartbreaking Visit to Child Labor Sweatshops," World of Good Development Organization, June 28, 2007, WorldofGood.org.

Michael C. Dorf   "What Constitutional Rights Should Schoolchildren Have? Two Recent Cases Underscore the Ways in Which Children Are Not Simply Miniature Adults," Findlaw.com, March 23, 2009.

Nancy Gibbs   "Birth Control for Kids?" *Time*, October 18, 2007.

Ryan Grim   "Blowing Smoke: Why Random Drug Testing Doesn't Reduce Student Drug Use," Slate.com, March 21, 2006.

Jennifer Haberkorn and S.A. Miller   "GAO Details Abuse Cases in Schools," *Washington Times*, May 20, 2009.

Benjamin Hess   "Children in the Fields: An American Problem," Association of Farmworker Opportunity Programs, May 2007.

Jesse J. Holland   "Savana Redding Strip Search Was Illegal, Supreme Court Says," *Huffington Post*, June 25, 2009.

Valerie Huber   "Opposing View: Best Message Is Abstinence," *USA Today*, September 3, 2008.

Hilary Hylton   "Texas Eases 'Zero Tolerance' Laws," *Time*, October 5, 2009.

Aaron Igdalsky   "Middle School Birth Control Is Absurd," *Daily Campus*, October 23, 2007.

Steph Kenrose   "The Case for Comprehensive Sex Education in Schools," Associated Content, July 29, 2009.

Jennifer Kern   "Drug Testing Students Counterproductive," *Seattle PI*, January 15, 2008.

Deborah Kotz   "A Debate About Teaching Abstinence," *US News & World Report*, December 19, 2007.

Tony Leys   "Uganda: Healing Former Child Soldiers," *Des Moines Register*, February 14, 2010.

Lindsay Lyon   "7 Reasons Parents Should Not Test Kids for Drug Use," *US News & World Report*, August 6, 2008.

Claire Morgenstern   "Ten Things You Should Know About Sex Education," Causecast.org, 2009.

Carolyn Moynihan   "Adults Still Trample Children's Rights: Abusive Institutions Have Closed Where Children Were Mistreated but Adults Still Abuse Children," *Spero News*, June 28, 2009.

Bill Muehlenberg   "Adult Selfishness, Child Suffering," BillMuehlenberg.com, July 16, 2009.

National Institute on Drug Abuse | "Frequently Asked Questions About Drug Testing in Schools," DrugAbuse.gov, September 2007.

Diana Philip | "Parental Involvement Laws: Why We Should Still Care That They Don't Work," Reproductive Health Reality Check, July 27, 2009, RHRealityCheck.org.

Luke Pryor | "In Defense of Sweatshops," *Cornell Daily Sun*, October 27, 2009.

Anna Quindlen | "Let's Talk About Sex," *Newsweek*, March 7, 2009.

Jennifer Riley | "Study: Abstinence Education Reduces Sexual Activity," *Christian Post*, February 3, 2010.

Mallory Simon | "My Bullied Son's Last Day on Earth," CNN.com, April 24, 2009.

Eileen Smolyar | "Lamb Chop, Sexual Education, and Birth Control Don't Go Together," *The Justice*, November 6, 2007.

Laura Sessions Stepp | "Study Casts Doubt on Abstinence-Only Programs," *Washington Post*, April 14, 2007.

Lindsay Tanner | "Study: Abstinence Program Might Work," Associated Press, February 2, 2010.

Ceil Than | "Facing the Bully in the Computer: What Is Cyberbullying?" Children's Rights of New York, Inc. *HOTLINE*, Vol. 29, No. 1, page 4, Spring 2008.

Ceil Than   "Mean Girls Have Two Faces: How to Recognize Girl-to-Girl Bullying," Children's Rights of New York, Inc. *HOTLINE*, Vol. 29, No. 1, page 7, Spring 2008.

Dan K. Thomasson "One Justice Failed to See the Obvious," *San Diego Union Tribune*, July 9, 2009.

Greg Toppo   "Restraint Can Dispirit and Hurt Special-Ed Students," *USA Today*, May 18, 2009.

United Nations Children's Fund "Female Genital Mutilation/Cutting: A Statistical Exploration," November 2005.

Ian Urbina   "It's a Fork, It's a Spoon, It's a . . . Weapon?" *New York Times*, October 11, 2009.

Rebecca Webber, J. Scott Orr, and Brooke Lea Foster "Should Schools Use Restraints on Students?" *Parade Magazine*, July 26, 2009.

Elizabeth Weil   "Teaching Boys and Girls Separately," *New York Times*, March 2, 2008.

Tiffany Ranae Widdifield "Should Kids in Middle School Have Access to Birth Control? Only If You Consider Yourself a Responsible Parent," Associated Content, October 18, 2007.

Michael Winerip "Drawing the Line on Drug Testing," *New York Times*, November 19, 2008.

Index